PROVIDENCE MY GUIDE

PROVIDENCE MY GUIDE

The heroic force in the Knock Shrine Story

Dame Judy Coyne

edited by Ethna Kennedy

MERCIER PRESS

First published in 2004 by
Mercier Press
Douglas Village, Cork
Email: books@mercierpress.ie
Website: www.mercierpress.ie

Trade enquiries to CMD Distribution
55A Spruce Avenue, Stillorgan Industrial Park
Blackrock, County Dublin
Tel: (01) 294 2560; Fax: (01) 294 2564
E-mail: cmd@columba.ie

© Ethna Kennedy, 2004

ISBN 1 85635 434 2
10 9 8 7 6 5 4 3 2 1

A CIP record for this title is available
from the British Library

Cover design by SPACE
Printed in Ireland by ColourBooks, Baldoyle Industrial Estate, Dublin 13

Mercier Press receives financial assistance from
the Arts Council/An Chomhairle Ealaíon

CONTENTS

Editor's note

On 8 September 1988, the late Dame Judy Coyne decided that she must write her memoirs. This was something she had always avoided doing, but I believe at that point somebody whose judgement she valued persuaded her that she must do so. I also believe, to quote her often repeated words that 'Providence intervened', as had she decided otherwise, we would never have heard this incredible account of how she and her husband, Judge Liam Coyne, against unbelievable odds, revived an interest in the then almost forgotten shrine at Knock, and brought it to what it is today, one of the principal Marian shrines in the world.

Over the years, I have taken down her story as she told it. Several of the anecdotes will already be well known to some of the handmaids at Knock and to a few close friends in whom she confided. During the telling, these stories never varied, they were given in great detail, with vibrant colour, wit and humanity. With amazing clarity of mind, she drew an extraordinary historical picture of conditions prevailing at Knock, and she continued to do so until the end of 2001, almost to the end of her life, when she felt she had said enough. However, practically every story told by her with apparent satisfaction and joy had its own sub-text of pain.

She was a deeply religious woman whose whole life was a prayer and whose charity was boundless. Her great love of God and Our Lady was reflected in her every deed. Shortly after the papal visit in 1979 she was awarded the medal 'Pro Ecclesia et Pontifice' the highest honour then available to a woman. When in 1997, Dr Michael Neary, Archbishop of Tuam, conferred on her the honour 'Dame Commander of the Order of St Sylvester', never before conferred on any woman in Ireland, she accepted it with reluctance, stipulating that it was being accepted also on behalf of the handmaids, stewards and promoters at Knock.

Her humility was extraordinary and she shunned publicity. Had others achieved the impossible, as she had so often done, they would have let the whole world know, but she always faded quietly into the background unnoticed. Nobody will be ever able to assess the enormous contribution she and her husband, Liam – and for the past fifty years, she alone – made to Knock. It would be impossible to quantify, but as she so often said herself, 'God knows, and that's all that matters'.

Ethna Kennedy
Bridgemount, June 2003

Introduction

People often ask me to tell them about my early memories of Knock shrine, of how I first became involved in working there, and in particular, of the part I have played in its development down the years. To each of these questions I can honestly reply that if anything ever happened by chance, that did. At the same time, I am convinced that there is no such thing as chance and there is always a reason for everything, so perhaps it was all meant to be. It began a very long time ago, so long ago in fact, that few will remember, but it all remains so vividly in my mind that it is never necessary for me to refer to the hundreds of letters from bishops, priests and laity to bring it to life. I have never told my story before, and it is only now, after a lifetime's work at Knock, and in response to a great deal of persuasion, that I have decided to do so. I do this very reluctantly, as it has always been my policy to keep silent on personal matters, and as a result, only those who were very close to the heart of things were aware at any time of developments. The decision to avoid publicity was taken at a very early stage, and my husband, Liam, and myself observed it at all times. However, I accept that it is important to give a full account of our work from the beginning, as without it, the story of Knock's extraordinary development would be incomplete. Above all else, and this is something that I would like to stress, I have always had a firm conviction that Providence guided our every step. Were it not for that Providence, perhaps this story could not now be told.

Judy Coyne
Bridgemount, December 2001

1

Childhood memories of Knock
First meaningful visit – 1929
Nationwide campaign

I remember being taken to Knock as a very young child, usually during August or September each year, together with sisters and brothers who were close to my own age. It was one of the big events of our childhood summers, and it came around as regularly as the buds on the trees or the first berries on the branches. It was a treat to be talked about for weeks in advance as our treats in those days were few. When the day came at last, we, the lucky ones whose turn it was to be taken, were washed from head to foot, our hair was brushed until it shone and then we were dressed up in our best. Eventually, when all the preparations had been carried out to everybody's satisfaction, we were packed into the trap behind the bay mare – whose harness always seemed to be gleaming in the sunshine – and off we would go at high speed over the hill, full of expectation for the big adventure.

Once we had arrived at Knock, an elder brother, or maybe a sister, depending on which of them had driven us, would help us to climb down, and would take the mare away to be fed, while we settled down to the serious business of praying. There were always endless rosaries, or so it seemed to me then, and we all had to take on our share in their recitation, though my particular sharing at the ripe age of four or maybe five, was more to show off my mastery of the words, than attention to their meaning. There were so many new things to wonder at, and big adventures to be considered, that praying was not of prime importance. I remember heaps of loose stones around the grounds, big lumpy stones, probably left over from some repair job, and inevitably there were smaller ones on which we scuffed our sandals. Here and there among the stones, pools of water, reminders of a recent shower, tempted our restless feet, but I don't think any particular fuss was made about sandals either scuffed or wet, as we trailed slowly round the church behind our elders.

Then, the praying done, we were taken to a shop on the hill, a reward for good behaviour! Three or four pairs of eyes would watch very closely as the woman who owned the shop reached to a shelf for a shiny can and weighed soft sugary sweets into a large brown paper bag, while she chatted to our mother and the others about the weather or the news of the moment. I was the youngest of a big family so nobody took much notice of me, and I stood there, my head barely reaching the counter, while I surveyed the scene and took in every detail. The smell of biscuits filled the shop, treacly sweet and slightly musty, but to me they were mouth watering delicacies, fat and round and as big as saucers, with a liberal sprinkling of currants on top. Anticipation of that moment, of sweets, biscuits and, maybe, if things were specially good, lemonade, was the highlight of my outing to Knock, and I could then set out for home quite satisfied with my lot.

In those days, Knock was a straggling village in the heart of Mayo, with a few houses, a few shops, a school, and a church on the hill. At the time we first became really aware of it, fifty years had elapsed since that blessed evening of 21 August 1879, when at about eight o'clock, with rain falling heavily and the light already fading, a wonderful Vision was seen on the gable of the parish church. The central figure was Our Lady, clothed all in white in a gown that fell ungirdled from throat to hem, her hands were raised to shoulder height in prayer and her expression was the rapt ecstasy of contemplation. On her head she wore a sparkling golden crown which held in place, in the centre of her fore-head, a single golden rose. To her right stood St Joseph with hands joined, his bowed head bent towards her. To her left was St John the Evangelist, wearing bishop's robes with a low mitre, unlike any seen before in Ireland. In his left hand was a book with a page held open, from which he seemed to preach, though no words were spoken. At the centre of the gable stood an altar supporting a lamb and behind the lamb, there was a large plain cross around which angels' wings were seen to hover. The Apparition lasted for about two hours during which time the gable, or the area surround-ing the figures, was bathed in an extraordinary light, des-cribed by one of the witnesses as something like the light of the moon.

Fifteen people of all ages, men, women and children saw this unique Vision, as they prayed aloud through the drenching rain. News of this extraordinary event quickly spread, as did tidings of subsequent cures and favours. Daily papers in Ireland and England carried the reports and crowds flocked to Knock. The excitement was so intense that six weeks afterwards, Dr MacHale, Archbishop of Tuam, set up a Commission of Enquiry. Each of the fifteen witnesses was examined and the Church authorities took depositions. The depositions were reported by the commission as being 'trust-worthy and satisfactory'.

Fifty years however, is a long time, and in that period very little had been done to either 'approve or disprove' the authenticity of Knock, so inevitably, precise information about it had become sketchy.

Shortly after I was married, some Dublin friends wrote one day and asked me and my husband, Liam, if we would meet them at Knock on a certain day. We wondered why they

13

had chosen Knock, but as they had told us it was going to be a very special occasion, and more particularly, as they were old family friends, we decided to go and thought no more about it. Eventually the day came. It was 15 August 1929, and we drove over to meet them as arranged. By that time, the motorcar had become a reality and I had learned to drive, but as yet cars were rare. We soon discovered that it was the golden jubilee of the Apparition, and there was what seemed to be quite a big pilgrimage from Dublin present. The weather that day was warm and very inviting, and the parish priest, Fr John Tuffy, had decided to hold the ceremonies in the open air, as the church was too small to accommodate the crowds. Dr Gilmartin was Archbishop of Tuam at the time, and he also had come for the ceremonies. I don't suppose any of us thought it unusual that the archbishop was present, or that he should just casually stand up on the Calvary – the elevated group of statues representing the crucifixion – to preach, we certainly didn't, and anyway, if he had wanted to be either seen or heard, there wasn't much else he could have done. In those days I knew little or nothing about bishops, in fact I had probably seen a bishop only once or twice before, at confirmation, and possibly at boarding school, but I remember thinking how splendid he looked as he stood there in his long purple robes and flowing lace, a brilliant dash of colour against the blue sky.

I, and the rest of our party moved near to the Calvary and edged our way close to him so we could hear what he had to say – there were no public address systems in those days. In the course of his homily, he told us that we must not take his presence there that day as giving official recognition to the Apparition alleged to have taken place fifty years before. For his part, he said, it should be understood that the Church had never given any opinion for or against it, and the commission which had been appointed to investigate it at the time had come to no positive conclusion. His words surprised us somewhat, but then we had never given Knock or the Apparition any serious consideration. It was not the sort of thing one normally analysed in youth, and although we knew the story – more or less – there had never been any reason to question its authenticity. However, the archbishop's words that day set us thinking, and as we drove home that evening, we asked ourselves why it was that we, and probably many others like us, knew so little about it. But there our questioning ended and, for the moment, we forgot all about it.

Reporting on the events of that day, one short sentence in a local newspaper, *The Connaught Telegraph*, made an interesting comment on the social conditions prevailing at the time, and gave an idea of the isolation of Knock and indeed the whole county, when it said, 'Dublin girls in short skirts and silk stockings contrasted with the homely attire of the west'. The 'homely attire' was significant of the way of life in those parts, where there was little contact with the outside world, and where much poverty remained. It seems almost impossible to believe now, but so it was.

The following year, 1930, we went to the Rue de Bac, the miraculous medal shrine in Paris for their centenary celebrations. Presumably, it was something that appealed to us at that particular time, but I don't remember the precise motivation. Having visited the shrine, we, like most visitors to Paris, went to the principal places of interest there. I was young and as I have always loved nice clothes, I could not resist spending hours in the shops admiring the stunning fashions, then all so new to me, and naturally I had to buy some outfits for myself. We went to visit the home of a relatively new saint, St Teresa of Lisieux, who was very much talked about around that time and whose simple life story had captured people's imagination. We stayed near her home in Lisieux, at that time not much more than a village, but it was an ideal place to make our headquarters for a few days. From there we drove around the quiet countryside, enjoying the novelty of it all, and particularly the superb French food which was so easily available even in remote and rural areas. My husband, Liam spoke French pretty well, so this sort of peaceful exploration was wonderful, and a completely new experience for me. The exchange rate with the franc was then very favourable to us, and we certainly made the most of it and of everything connected with our time there.

As it so happened, we had travelled out to Paris with some Irish nuns who were members of the French Sisters of Charity at the Rue de Bac. From them we learned that a few of their sisters were in the process of going to Knock, to take over their newly acquired house there, the house now known as St Mary's Hostel. At that stage, we knew nothing about the hostel, but we promised the sisters that we would go and visit when we got back. Knock was a bleak assignment for them in those days, they had few comforts and little to brighten their lives. Also, as the number of pilgrims was then very small, their whole future there was uncertain, and it remained so for quite some time. Shortly after our return, we called as promised and we soon got to know them very well. In the months, and indeed the years, that followed, we went there regularly, usually taking flowers in season and helping the sister in charge to decorate Our Lady's altar in the church. Off and on during that time, we tried to find out more about the Apparition, and as we learned about it, we wondered why it was not better known – but our questions still prompted no action.

It was not until we went on a pilgrimage to Lourdes in 1934, almost four years later, and became conscious of the extraordinary devotion of the pilgrims there to Our Blessed Lady that we began, in some unexplained way, to compare it with Knock. We were deeply impressed by the quiet prayerfulness during the masses at the grotto, and the pervading reverence at all times. Above all else, I was greatly moved by the blessing of the sick with the Blessed Sacrament, which we saw there for the first time. While the prayers were being given out, a bishop moved through the rows and rows of invalids, blessing them with the Host, and as they responded to each invocation, the fervour of that response was almost tangible. It was as if nothing else on this earth mattered to them and it was a tremendous testament of faith. Above any other ceremony at Lourdes, that personal blessing of the sick made the deepest impression on us. Each day we joined in the huge processions, each one made up of large numbers of pilgrims from every country in Europe, and as we did so, we asked ourselves again and again why we were not seeing the same thing happening at Knock. After all, we reasoned, it was the same Blessed Mother in both places, and the Apparition at Knock seemed to be so full of meaning. A strange feeling of a need to do something to promote it began to nag at both my husband and myself, and there was no getting rid of it. Apart from the devotional side, we were also very much aware of the big number of invalids who had travelled with us on our pilgrimage, and we could imagine the physical effort, not to mention the financial commitment, it had taken to get them there. How much easier it would be for all concerned, we reasoned, if they could be taken to a shrine at home.

One evening, towards the end of our stay, while we stood watching the candlelight procession, these thoughts were foremost in our minds. As it drew to a close, we spoke to two young priests from our own diocese, Fr Peter Kelly and Fr Larry Lyons who were standing near to us, and asked them why we were not seeing the same crowds and processions at Knock. They listened to what we had to say, and we talked about it with them for quite some time, but none of us could come up with a satisfactory answer. On our return journey a day or two later, quite by chance we shared the same railway carriage and, without knowing why, as we certainly had no prior intention of doing so, we returned to the subject of Knock and asked them again how we might go about making it better known. By that time we had more or less acknowledged to ourselves that this was something we must do, but we did not yet see how we might go about it. Our train sped homeward on the long journey across France and by the end of our very long talk, they were of the opinion that nothing could be achieved during the lifetime of the archbishop, Dr Gilmartin, as they felt that he was too 'conservative'. It seemed to be a disappointing end to a session of earnest questioning, but time was to prove otherwise.

Soon after our return home, an old and valued friend, Anita McMahon, came to stay with us. Anita was from a Cork family and was closely related to Daniel O'Connell. She had been educated abroad and was a fluent linguist. When I first met her, she had translated several books and was full of admiration for the new generation of Irish writers, Yeats, Synge, Lady Gregory and all the others, as well as writers in the Irish language. She had been one of the original members of the Gaelic League when it was founded in Dublin and had known T. W. Rolleston and Yeats. By that time, Liam had known her for several years and had a very high opinion of her.

As a university student in Germany towards the end of the Great War, Liam, classified a British subject, had been imprisoned for a time. The outcome of the war was then becoming apparent to the Germans, and the finer points of enemy boundaries were not important; being Irish in those days meant being British. The ironic twist occurred when, shortly after his escape from Germany and his safe return home, he was imprisoned yet again, this time by the British. Their charge against him then was that he was a nationalist. Being a nationalist in that context merely meant that he had a great love for Ireland and all things Irish. Sometime during those troubled years, he had met Anita, who, a nationalist more or less to the same degree, had also been imprisoned. After all of that, when the country had settled down to some kind of normal living under self government, Anita had worked for several years to improve the lot of the people of Achill Island, and had helped to establish craft industries and various schemes there which were ideal for the well being of the people. Aside from her literary and organising talents, her love of God and neighbour was quite extraordinary, a quality which I found in her repeatedly.

Around that time, together with other Mayo people, Liam and I worked on the committee of a project which we called the 'Mayo Industrial Development Organisation'. This was intended to foster home industry, which meant cottage industry of all types, knitting, weaving, leatherwork, pottery, bee and poultry keeping, and it was all to be carried out to the highest possible standards. On that committee we had Col Maurice Moore, one of the Moores of Moore Hall and brother of the writer George. Although his home, with its priceless library, had been ruthlessly burned in the political frenzy that had gone before, he still had the welfare of his county and its people at heart. We had James Fitzgerald Kenny of Clogher, a prominent barrister, who, with all his family, was very much to the fore in county affairs. There was Eva O'Flaherty, who had founded the St Colman's knitting industry in Keel, a factory which was then producing beautiful, personally designed knitwear, of a standard equal to or maybe even more imaginative than any top designer knitwear available today; and there was Anita, who had probably more organising ability than all of us together.

Among many events that year we organised a very successful fancy dress ball in aid of Irish industry in the then
new and very much admired 'Maple Hall' in Balla, with Stephen Garvey's 'Augmented' Dance Band, and the Hibernian
Orchestra from Ballina to play for the dancing. Stephen
Garvey's was then probably the top band in the country,
and a night with him playing was guaranteed quality. The
venue may not sound very exciting today, but it was then
the place to be, and when it was finally ready for the evening, its maple floor gleaming like satin and banked with
masses of fresh spring flowers, white tablecloths and pretty
lights, it was, in our eyes anyway, quite on a par with the
Ritz. Long before the notion of inviting VIPs became an
established promotional practice, we got some very important people, or people who might be useful in some way to
our organisation, to attend, and we also got splendid prizes
from various firms, to be given for the best costumes depict-
ing an Irish historical personality or theme. The ball was a
huge social and financial success. For months in advance it
was talked about as the main social event of the west, and
it earned a great deal of good will for our work.

The development project did not survive however,
mainly because of apathy on the part of shopkeepers who
found higher profit margins in imported goods. I remember
one amusing incident that happened in Westport where I
was known for my connections with the organisation. One
day during one of our 'Buy Irish' promotions, I was glancing
casually into a shop window there wondering how many of
the items on display had, in fact, been made in Ireland; it
wasn't much of a window display and the goods seemed
shoddy. Then the owner spotted me and retreated rapidly.
Just as rapidly, a hand appeared pushing a handwritten notice, the ink still wet, to the front of the window bearing
the legend, 'Everything in this window was made in Ire-

land'. I don't think that particular claim would have stood up to much serious investigation.

Alongside that attitude of indifference, there was a dismal response from government ministers, who were more preoccupied with election tactics within the new state. There was also the notion that no ideas should be put forward by any region outside Dublin and, above all, they must never come from that backward and benighted place, the west. Today, semi-state bodies work on lines very similar to those we tried to pioneer, while government grants give substantial aid to worthy rural projects. But in the early 1930s, the country was not yet ready for such self-promotion; the scheme was decades in advance of its time.

When Anita came to visit us again later that year, we told her about all we had been doing, and of our interest in Knock. Although she knew very little about it, she listened to all we had to say with great interest. After a few days, we took her to visit the shrine and, together, all three of us prayed at the gable. When we had finished our prayers, I said that I felt the presence of Our Lady there as strongly as I had felt it in Lourdes and, without any hesitation, she, who had also visited Lourdes a short time before, replied that she had experienced exactly the same feeling. That night we talked about it well into the small hours and, after much discussion, Anita encouraged us strongly to try to do something to promote it. All during the remainder of her time with us, we talked about nothing else. We knew that very little precise information was available about it, but even more important was the realisation that one or two of the witnesses were still alive, though they were getting old, while several other people remembered the event clearly. Time was of vital importance, and if anything at all was going to be done, we knew that the time had come to do it. Anita was older than either of us, and more experienced in handling difficult negotiations, so after more and still more discussion, we finally decided that the talking had to stop and a beginning had to be made.

The first thing we did was to visit Canon John Grealy, who was parish priest of Knock at the time, to talk to him about it, and generally to get his views. He welcomed us warmly, listened to all we had to say, and then, to our great relief, told us that he would help us in every way he could. As I look back now after so many years, I am very conscious of the fact that it was Canon Grealy above anybody else who first got us involved in working for Knock, and though we did not realise it at the time, he did so very soon after we first approached him.

We had no fixed plan of action at that stage, but having spoken to the canon at length, it was decided that we should approach the archbishop before we did anything else. As it so happened, Anita had an appointment to see him in the course of the following few days. In view of her past record, she seemed the obvious person to talk with him initially on our behalf. She had known him for several years and from what we could gather, he held her in high esteem. Some years before, she had been one of the main movers in getting a church built at Keel on Achill island. Until that time the only church on the island had been the one at Achill Sound, with a small chapel also at Dookinelly. At high tides and during Atlantic gales, the sea came across the road making access to Dookinelly almost impossible; while the journey all the way from Keel and the west to the Sound was, in the days of donkeys and carts or more likely on foot, difficult in the extreme, especially in winter. In such conditions, Sunday Mass was a genuine problem for a large number of the islanders. During those negotiations, which had been troublesome, Anita had played a major part successfully, and so she had easy enough access to the archbishop.

She was delighted to find the archbishop so sympathetic and so interested. He asked her to tell us that before anything could be done, the whole undertaking would have to have a great deal of prayer, and he advised us to put together a prayer leaflet. This seemingly simple direction from him was the beginning of endless planning; the draft leaflet went back and forward for comment between Anita and us for weeks. Anita, though rarely ill, was not what one might call robust, and she usually spent her winters in Switzerland or France, with occasional visits to Glengarrif in between. She was happy in Glengarrif and considered its climate to be suitable for her. When the question of Knock came up, she was working mostly from there. All too soon after that however, her poor health gave more serious cause for anxiety, and indeed before long took her completely out of the Knock scene.

We began to prepare the prayer leaflet on the lines the archbishop had indicated, which was to include a brief history of the shrine together with an account and picture of the Apparition, as well as some carefully selected prayers. The history of the shrine was something which we had already considered to be necessary, as from the beginning we had found it extremely difficult to discover precise information about it. Simple as all of this may sound today, it was to prove a most difficult task. As far as we knew at the time, there had been only one picture of the Apparition, the one given by Archbishop Murphy of Hobart in Tasmania years before in thanksgiving for having had his sight restored by the application of some of the old cement from the gable. By 1934, that picture was in tatters, its canvas mildewed from damp and disintegrating from the neglect of years. At one time, some line drawings had been made from it, but even though we knew about them, we had never seen them, and we had no idea of where we should even begin to look for them. We tried getting various artists to make a sketch from the description we gave them, but in those days it was difficult to get any artist to take such a request seriously. Having heard little, or more likely nothing, about the shrine, the suggestion was met with disbelief; they listened politely enough, but it soon became obvious that they were just tolerating some sort of religious crank. After numerous attempts, I found an artist in Galway who was willing to try, but being willing and actually doing something are very different things. I clearly remember making ten journeys there over a couple of weeks, and though he began with a reasonably acceptable image of Our Lady's head and shoulders, nothing I could do or say could get him to complete the picture, so I had to abandon the idea. Time was then getting short, and we were becoming almost desperate for some picture or sketch we could use.

One morning the post arrived and among the letters was one from Tom Maguire, the man who had organised the pilgrimage from Dublin to Knock in 1929 when we were there, and with whom we were then in correspondence. Enclosed with the letter was a very old Knock leaflet, and there, gazing at us from that leaflet, which was about the size of a postcard, were three old and faded photographs: the elusive drawing of Our Lady of Knock; the gable; and Archdeacon Cavanagh, parish priest at Knock at the time of the Apparition, at the door of his cottage. It seemed to us like a providential answer to our problem, something which encouraged us very much that morning.

After that, the delays in the preparation of the leaflet were minimal. It went back and forth between us and Anita, and then, when it was a bit more advanced, at the stage of the final meticulously prepared mock-up, we took it to Canon Grealy, who was to take it to the archbishop for his approval. In no time at all, however, he sent us a message to get the final printed leaflet to the archbishop ourselves, as he was about to come to a conference in Castlebar. This gave us barely a week or so to complete it.

On the appointed day, we went to Castlebar, wondering all along the way how we might be received in view of the 'conservative' image of Dr Gilmartin, then firmly fixed in our minds. However, one doesn't always find as expected: we found the archbishop to be a quiet, reserved, almost an aloof man, but he was most kindly, with an air of old-world courtesy. Through the months and indeed years that were to follow, and as we got to know him better, we discovered him to be a thorough gentleman. That day Liam gave him the leaflet and I remember how slowly he read it, thinking over each sentence most carefully. Then, having done so, he said with a smile, 'Go ahead now and promote it'.

The words seemed simple enough then, and we little dreamed of the task that lay before us.

We began by sending a copy of the prayer leaflet to every enclosed order of nuns in Ireland, England, Scotland and even to some in America to ask for their prayers for the success of the cause of Knock. We also visited other convents in Ireland to give them copies and to request that the children in their schools would offer the Angelus every day asking for Our Lady's blessing on our work. Half a million of those leaflets were distributed free of charge in the first year, and in the doing, we drove hundreds of miles up and down the country. In those days, every town in the country had a convent, often two or even more, each with a large number of nuns. Between them, they also had big schools, so we would have been reaching thousands of children and, we hoped, getting their prayers. Covering all of them required very precise planning. We would set out whenever we could find the time: if we could fit in a journey on a day between Liam's courts – Liam worked as a judge – we did so, frequently he had to take some of his annual leave to get to the more distant places; and if he could not possibly take the time, I went alone. From that summer on, annual leave was something which came to be used entirely for the promotion of Knock. Holidays in the accepted sense were a luxury that we had to forget about. Each autumn we, like most people, were full of plans to go here or there in the coming summer, but when the time came, there was always something else which required our attention.

Distributing those leaflets was an enormous undertaking in driving time alone, especially in those days when cars were not as reliable as they are today and one might have serious mechanical problems at any time. However, we both managed to cope without anything more serious than the occasional spell of total exhaustion.

As part of our campaign we began to enlist people from all walks in life to pray for the Cause of Knock, requesting them to recite simple prayers, one Our Father, one Hail Mary, one Gloria and the Memorare daily, and if possible, to offer one Holy Communion. We also asked those who were in a position to do so to spread a true knowledge of the shrine through the distribution of shrine literature, helping organise pilgrimages and encouraging invalids to visit. Foreseeing inevitable development, we asked all those signing up to contribute a modest sum, just a few cents today, to cover the costs of printing and general expenses. This practice developed rapidly and before long it was possible to provide loudspeakers – a necessary facility when dealing with crowds – the outdoor stations of the cross, and in due course, an outside altar, but all of that was still in the future. The successful enlistment of members came about through the work of promoters, all volunteers, who would get together a list of five or more names, and for whom in turn, we had special Masses offered at the shrine. The names of these promoters were listed in the first *Knock Shrine Annual*, classified by county, or even country, and they have been, and continue to be, the backbone of all funding for Knock Shrine Society for almost seventy years.

The operation was not without its lighter moments. It is hard to believe now that Knock was almost unknown even in some parts of Ireland in those days. I remember ringing at doorbells in various convents and trying to tell the sister who came to answer, and who now and then eyed us with some suspicion, our reason for wanting to see the superior. When we finally got to the reverend mother, or whoever might have been in charge, our opening words invariably were, 'We haven't come to ask for money, but we would like to ask for your prayers'. In the end, when we had said all we had to say, the sister, who by that time was no longer suspicious of the intruders, would often call in other sisters, sometimes the whole community, to meet us. Then when the ice had been broken and formalities were laid aside, the nuns frequently told us many things that were new to us, particularly their own experiences of Knock before they entered the convent. Several remembered looking through a peephole in a small wooden cross which showed the village church on one side and Archdeacon Cavanagh on the other. That small cross was for years the definitive souvenir of Knock, one of the very first that I myself remember, even as a child, and, though similar in design to various key-ring attachments and other picture-bearing objects common today, I suppose it was very sophisticated for its time.

As it turned out, calling on the convents led us to valuable information relating to cures of which the sisters had personal experience, very often through contact which they had kept up with past pupils, many of whom were emigrants. I remember in particular a visit to a Presentation convent in Co. Kerry where they told us a most extraordinary story about one of their pupils. In the chilling poverty of former times, she had emigrated to some remote region of America, having been sent the money for her fare by a brother or sister who had gone before her. This was a common enough custom then, one went first, then saved enough money to send the price of a ticket to the next, and so it went on. There, strange to tell, and it was a story we thought so impossible that we had it verified at the time, she had contracted leprosy; indeed it had progressed so far that she had to resort to covering her disfigured face with a veil when her brothers came to visit her. After some time, somebody by chance sent her some of the old cement from the Apparition gable, and in applying it, she promised that she would return to Knock to give thanks if cured. Miraculously, the dreaded disease left her and she did come back. But she wanted to do more than just give thanks, so on her return to America, she entered a convent from where, in full health, she wrote to the Kerry nuns regularly. Several of them had first hand information about that particular cure, and as she had died only a short time before our visit there, they were clear about its every detail.

We usually came away from those convents feeling much better from our talk, always carrying with us a promise of prayers and most helpful words of encouragement. This prayerful support was something on which we knew we could rely, an added blessing which those nuns certainly gave us in good measure throughout those very early years.

2

Bridgemount: life there and background
Society founded – 1935
First members of Society
Handmaids

L iam and I had not been married very long at that time, and we were gradually settling down to that new phase in our lives, which to us was, naturally, a great adventure. The courts, to which Liam had been appointed as judge, had not then been long established within the new Free State. They followed a period of great unrest after its foundation, and the back-log of work was enormous. On leaving home each morning he could hardly ever tell me when I might expect him home for dinner, as they often sat all day and well into the night. In the circumstances, meal planning was a perpetual problem and so it remained for several years. It was not only meal planning that was difficult, the whole framework of the courts and their organisation demanded considerable thought and consultation. This, in turn, meant many hours outside the official ones, and to the end of his days, there were always the occasions when an on the spot emergency case had to be heard to its conclusion whatever the hour. It all added up to a marathon task for several years. Despite all that, he found the life interesting and satisfying, with more than enough to occupy his mind completely, and he was very content.

After a lengthy spell of house hunting, we found Bridge-mount, or Bridgemount House as it was then called. There was not a great deal of suitable property to choose from in this part of Mayo at the time, but it was central enough to all the courts and the house seemed to have possibilities. It was at the time when the whole question of land ownership was very contentious in the west, and steps were being taken to increase the holdings of smaller farmers to make them viable. By that time land was being taken from the bigger farmers by the land commission if it was considered that their farms were in excess of their immediate family's requirements, and they were then given a farm in exchange in the less heavily populated parts of Counties Dublin, Meath or Kildare. Bridgemount and its lands were one such holding, and already a large portion of it had been divided among local people. We bought the house from the land commission who offered us the statutory number of acres, but we decided against buying land which we didn't need and settled for a couple of paddocks, together with the large orchard and room to make a decent garden. It was a neat and well-defined little parcel of ground, with a river running by the gate, its own neat gate-house on one of its sides, and a small stream on the other; all considered, sufficient for our requirements.

A family called Acton had owned the place, in fact at the time we bought it they were still living in the house, making final arrangements for their move to Co. Dublin and waiting for their new house to be built. The son of the house, George, then a man in his fifties, I suppose, thought nothing of setting out on his motorbike for a performance of the opera in Dublin during the season. The journey seemed to be of no consequence to him, and he spoke to us about it with enthusiasm and pride, almost as if it might prove to be a selling point for the house.

The house was situated about seven miles from Castlebar in quiet rolling countryside, a mile from Belcarra village. When we first moved, our plan was to refurbish the house to the standards of comfort of the day. Structurally it was in excellent condition, but it had been built in early Victorian times and needed a fair bit of modernisation. We got plumbers and decorators to come from Dublin, and they stayed on in the house for months and months while they laid on running water, and re-did everything from basement to roof. Mrs Acton had used white hand-made wallpaper in the dining-room and the door panels were painted in oils with flowers and other Victorian motifs. The wallpaper, though very impressive, I thought to be too cold looking, and, however much my decision might be frowned on today, I had something that I considered warmer and more practical hung instead. Together we went to auctions and shopped on the quays and in antique shops in Dublin for suitable furniture – which was easy enough to find and reasonably priced in those days – and we soon had enough for our needs.

Around that time also, Pat Burke, who had been for some years working for my uncle, P. K. Joyce, in Hazelrock near Westport, wrote to me one day and asked if he could come to us permanently to work. Uncle P. K., like so many others, had had to move to Dublin. Pat, who had moved with him, disliked the frequent trips he had to make into city traffic, though I cannot imagine it being very hectic in those days. As it so happened, Bridgemount was also only a half hour's drive from his old home, which gave him an extra reason for wanting to come. Liam and I both knew Pat pretty well at that stage; he had been around with Uncle P. K. at Hazelrock for as long as I could remember. Many a time he had caught and saddled hunters for me when as a young girl I had stayed with my aunt and uncle there, and delighted in riding all over the picturesque countryside. So he came and stayed with us, and became very much part of our lives and of the household. Indeed, Pat has his own place in the whole of the Knock story, he was around to help in the practical things at all hours of the day and night, always lightening difficult moments with his droll and ready wit. His death some years ago was a very great sadness to me.

Soon after Pat's arrival we bought a small pony and cart and, with the help of a couple of neighbouring lads, he excavated the field, as it then was, in front of the house, and built terraces on two levels. It was hard work for man and pony all those years ago, long before the days of the JCBs, but they took it on cheerfully, and in a year or two the new young lawns were beautiful with smooth green grass. Then in the low double walls which Pat had built, we planted hundreds of bulbs and laid out a tennis court on one side of the centre path and a croquet lawn on the other. In no time at all the gardens were a blaze of colour stretching out in front of the house as they fell away towards the river. It was a beautiful sight on a fine evening in summer, often with a crimson sky behind at sunset, and in the distance on a hill, the crumbling ruin of an old castle. At that time also, we planted rows of cypresses and conifers, which were decorative and beautiful for years, but in the course of time grew to be very tall trees and blocked out the view. It is a fact that one can rarely have everything, but as a bonus, they provide invaluable shelter for the house, particularly when the wind blows from the west.

Above all else – it was something which we scarcely realised at the time, but gradually as we came to recognise it, it became extremely important to both of us – the house possessed an extraordinary sense of tranquillity. Hidden from the road by tall beech trees, and approached by a tree-lined winding drive, one is immediately conscious of its compelling peace and serenity. Even today, when I return from a difficult meeting or an otherwise stressful appointment, or maybe just from a heavy day's work at the shrine, it is easy to shut off all tension and find complete renewal in its almost tangible silence. Now and then people say to me, 'Are you never lonely in that house, so far away from everything and everybody?' But to that question I can truly reply that never, in all the years I have lived here, have I felt either lonely or nervous. On the contrary, here I find rest, and in such close communion with nature, it is easy to be in touch with God, and see Him in its beauty. I have always felt that the grace of God is very close to me in this house. This is something which grew with us in those early years, and it is precious to me now, it is more than that, it is a quality that is for me, beyond price.

During my days at boarding school, I had organised a lot of tennis, and had grown to love it. I played it regularly and, when I left school, I played in numerous tournaments before I was married, then Liam and I continued to play together. Sometimes our friends and families came to join us, or sometimes they came just to sit in the shade of the sweet-smelling sycamores and have tea. I wonder if everybody remembers the long sunny days of youth! The orchard was also a delight. The Actons in their time had employed a few men to look after it, and, as the seasons came and went, we gradually discovered – apart from the dozens of splendid apple trees – gooseberries, black and red currants, raspberries, loganberries and all sorts of fruits, which, protected by high stone walls, flourished in abundance. Some of the apples were delicious, as Acton, who did all his farming and gardening on scientific lines, had been constantly experimenting and endeavouring to produce new strains, often with wonderful results. Between the trees, there was a wealth of summer flowers, beautiful for cutting. However, as several men had always tended the orchard, it soon became obvious that we could not possibly give it the attention required to keep it at such a level of excellence. At first, we were able to cope with it, up to a point, but as the

Knock work took over, there was no more spare time and, apart from collecting the fruit in season, which we did for quite a while, it had to look after itself.

For a few years after buying the house, we enjoyed it to the full, and looked forward to a continuing happy and peaceful lifetime here. In the evenings, the day's work done, if nobody happened to be staying with us, we would sometimes go for a walk along the bog road, or we might sit and listen to music. Liam was a good pianist, but above everything else, he loved to read. With this in mind, we had one large room off the hall made into a study, and in no time at all he and Pat had the walls shelved and lined with books which he bought from bookshops in Dublin and indeed anywhere else he could find them. He had a great passion for books, and it was almost impossible to get him away from bookshops, in particular from those with old and rare collections. Whenever we went to Dublin, he made a bee-line for the bookshops along the quays where he would spend hours. Bit by bit he acquired a useful collection, mostly on Irish affairs, as well as books in Irish, and on history, biography, literature and law.

I suppose one might consider all of this to have been an unlikely starting point for an all-out crusade for Knock, and in all honesty, I don't think that we envisaged any deep involvement at the time. It might take a couple of years, we thought, maybe even three or at most four, and then it would be taken up by those who appeared to be the obvious people to do it, and we could return to normal life. At no stage was it even dreamed of as a life-long commitment. Indeed, I clearly remember close family and friends being quite concerned, thinking us to be very unwise, when we finally decided to get involved and told them about our intention.

Very quickly, however, the house, which we had just begun to look on as a reasonably comfortable family home, took on a new dimension as the volume of work increased, and bit by bit, it became the centre of all activity for Knock. It is almost incredible now even to me, but it is a fact that for almost forty years all pilgrimages were booked and all other Knock business carried out from Bridgemount. That does not mean that the pilgrimages were fewer in those days, far from it, the Sunday pilgrimages grew quickly to huge proportions, and we were well into discussions about the centenary by the time that work was handed over to a central office at Knock. In all those years, from the moment the post was delivered to us in the morning, it was a frantic scramble to get the letters answered, and every enquiry dealt with. We didn't have the telephone until shortly after the war, but from the moment it was installed, during busy periods at the shrine, it rang almost incessantly. Four o'clock has always been, and still is, deadline for post collection in the village, but more often than not, when the post for that day had been collected, we typed on until late at night and even then we were lucky to get all letters dealt with before next day.

It amazes me now to recall, and it will certainly come as a surprise to many people, when they are told that for the same length of time, all food for the invalids and the helpers was provided, cooked, and taken to Knock from Bridgemount, and in those early years that was a very big number of people indeed. Even shopping for such quantities of food was a huge undertaking, which one planned and set out to complete as part of a day's work. It was quite normal for me to drive home from town on a Friday, the car laden down with provisions. I usually left my car parked somewhere in the main street in Castlebar, and went from there to various shops, in those days there were no parking restrictions for there were very few cars. It was also long before the days of supermarkets, so of necessity, shopping was rather fragmented. The car was left unlocked, and as each order was completed, the parcels – they were always parcels – wrapped in brown paper and tied with string, were sent along to it. Eventually, I would arrive back from my last port of call and check that everything had been delivered, then, satisfied that all was correct, I would drive home. It says much about society then, especially considering the widespread poverty prevailing, that in all those years, nothing was ever touched, or stolen, from that car.

Over the years, cooking methods have changed, and today one can plan to make things easier, there is pre-cooking, deep-freezing and a thousand other methods of food preparation. It was a different story in the 1930s, 1940s, and even into the 1960s and early 1970s. I shall always remember Fridays and Saturdays when the range and several independent boilers in kitchen and basement were full of simmering hams and legs of lamb, rarely less than ten, though frequently there were many more, tended by Pat and whoever else we might have had as house help at the time. By any standards, it was an immense undertaking, at the weekends the whole place became a huge cook-house, while all the time, the post and telephone were being dealt with, duty lists for helpers were being drafted and flowers for the statue and shrine were being cut, organised or collected.

In those days too, the roads were bad, there were no satisfactory shortcuts for cars, so one had to go through either Kiltimagh or Claremorris to get to Knock, which for us meant a journey each way of some twenty miles. Frequently, because of the difficulty in obtaining fresh food there on days of large pilgrimages, particularly milk, it was necessary to return home to get fresh supplies. Milk did not then come in tidy litres from creameries as it does today; its delivery, if there was any at all in rural areas, was very haphazard. Indeed there were times, especially for vigils, when Pat had to milk the cows and we would load up with fresh containers before we set out for Knock. One has to realise also that there was no refrigeration at that time, so perishable foods had to be used quickly and handled with great care.

On top of all that practical catering and organising strategy, all the publications by what was to become known as the Knock Shrine Society were dealt with in their entirety. That meant that alongside the *Annual* and various pamphlets, there were also the books. Dealing with them could have been a whole time job on its own, work for far more than two, as it meant taking on everything connected with the publications, research, arranging for copy, proofreading, photographs, and all the other time-consuming tasks that arise until the final print-off. Looking back now, even I, and thank God, I could always cope with a tidy workload, cannot imagine how it was done. I suppose it was possible only through having absolute trust in God, through relentless work to the total exclusion of everything else.

From the moment the house was ready we had friends come to stay with us, and naturally, we had some very good days with them, but from the mid-1930s on, people who were interested in Knock, or who could help us with its development in some way, were our main guests. Inevitably the character of those guests became different, and the tone of conversation changed, usually taking on a much more serious note. During those days there were several occasions when I must admit, near to despair, we would sometimes say, 'Why us, surely there must be others who could and should do this?' It was a normal reaction, I suppose, to situations which seemed so far removed from everything we had ever done. However, the compelling urge remained with each of us, and spurred us on. Liam was a very spiritual person who had a great love of God and Our Blessed Lady, and he felt that in helping to promote the shrine he was doing something worthwhile. As far as I am concerned, I know that from my first adult encounter with Knock I had a very strong conviction that we should do everything possible to promote it. I also felt that if we did not do it, nobody would, and perhaps I was right. That said, however, it was not a commitment we took on lightly, but only after a great deal of thought, of prayer for guidance and, I suppose one could reason, the necessity to do it, at least as we saw it.

As a result of our experiences while distributing the prayer leaflets, we had come to recognise the great desire that existed among a large number of people to find out about the shrine and to help in its promotion. It seemed almost as if they had been waiting for that moment, and as tidings of our work spread, more and more people came to us or wrote to tell us of their own personal Knock experience. All at once, it seemed, feelings that had been bottled up for years suddenly found expression and were spilling over. We were quickly coming to realise that because of this increasing volume of work at the shrine, the time had come to establish a recognised group of people to help with it.

Once again, we approached Canon Grealy and the archbishop; they appreciated our problem and suggested that we go ahead with our proposed plan to get others involved. Then, with their written permission – perhaps we were over cautious, but we always made a point of getting written permission from both parish priest and archbishop for everything we did – a society entitled 'Society for Promoting the Cause of Knock Shrine' was founded. That was in July 1935. The first meeting was held in the old Knock school house on 21 August that year with the few members we then had, present. Liam was elected president of the society and I was voted to be organising secretary. Over the course of years, the society became known as 'Knock Shrine Society' and as such it functions today.

Two months later at another meeting – which had a huge attendance – we sensed for the first time the importance of well-defined objectives, objectives which over the years laid out the development of the shrine. That October meeting was a public one to which many sections of the community were invited. A great deal of thought went into it and its agenda, as we knew that a big impact must be made and we were determined to get it right. In the short time we had then been working on Knock's promotion, we had been made aware all too often that the prevailing notion in many minds was that only the poor and the ignorant ever went there. We had by then found out as much as possible about the Apparition and recognised some aspects of its singular importance. We had spoken at great length about it with some open-minded priests and responsible members of the laity.

We gradually came to realise that in order to make more people understand its full significance, something had to be done to counteract the reality of its too often facile dismissal. At the same time, we appreciated the fact that it was the faith of the country people which had kept Knock alive during its waiting years. Speaking to a group of priests at Knock a few years ago, Fr Francis Sullivan, SJ, a theologian and then a university lecturer in Rome, referred in complimentary terms to the 'simple faithful' who saw and believed in the Vision at Knock, as indeed they had done in other places. We printed the talk in the 1992 *Knock Shrine Annual* as 'Vision of Contemplation'. It has always been in the nature of things that such 'simple faithful' need eloquent and influential advocates to state their case. With Knock, it was essential to invite such advocates – those well placed in positions of authority and known for an exemplary lifestyle, together with some who were experienced in religious matters – to join us.

At the time of that meeting, it was mainly a matter of making the true account of the Apparition known, and devising plans to promote it, so priests, county councillors, doctors, lawyers and the press were approached to attend. We had a great deal of genuine support at the time but inevitably, we had to endure our share of ridicule. Our main concern then was to conceive a plan to enhance the Apparition gable, at that time plain and unattractive, as well as to ensure the general preservation of the shrine and its precincts for future development. Arising out of that meeting various proposals for town planning were put forward by the Society to Mayo County Council. These proposals came up for discussion again and again right into the late 1940s, by which time most of them had been finally agreed upon, though by that time the war had created unprecedented shortages, and travel, because of fuel rationing, was very restricted. Apart from the predictable issues like roads and water, they included plans for improvements in the rail system, and an airfield. With air travel then in its infancy – a dream of the future for most people – that suggestion caused as much derision within its context as Knock Airport did in the 1980s. However, those plans, though maybe far-fetched for 1935, have, thank God, materialised.

Looking now at the names of those who formed the committee of that first society, is almost like looking at another world, indeed up to a point it was. Almost everybody forming it was considerably older than we were, and their wide and varied experience provided an invaluable store of knowledge. The intellectual and moral calibre of those early members was quite formidable, and they became powerful allies whenever Liam and I needed help or encouragement.

As vice-president, we had Senator Helena Concannon of Galway, a woman who had written several significant books on history and on religious affairs and who was, thank God, fearless when it came to helping Knock. In the early days of the *Knock Shrine Annual* she wrote, and arranged for others to write, fine and courageous articles for us at a time when one had to watch one's words very carefully. We had Michael Egan, then secretary of Mayo County Council and others of that calibre who were in a position to help, and who genuinely wanted to do so.

Notable also was Senator Eibhlin Costello from Tuam, wife of Dr Tom Costello, a medical doctor who had a practice in the town, and who was also a great historian. Now and then when some urgent matter needed to be discussed, we would call on them at their home in Tuam, and having been shown upstairs, would find them among their books, always ready to welcome us and to talk about Knock, as well as about current issues. Dr Costello usually sat in his large leather covered armchair, two of his sleek dachshunds asleep on his lap. At first, the dogs always raised a great alarm when we called, but they got to know us before long, and barely lifted a languid eyelid on being disturbed. Mrs Costello was an Englishwoman who had become a Catholic, and who, in her youth, had grown very enthusiastic about all things Irish, in particular the language. She had learned Irish from scratch, and in the days when Irish teachers were few, she was sufficiently proficient to teach it. She was also a very well known folk-song collector, whose book of songs, *Amhráin Mhuige Sheola*, was then widely used by schools and choral societies. I understand the original edition is now a collectors' item.

At that very first meeting it was decided to establish a body of helpers which, in due course, we called handmaids and stewards. The handmaids would help the sick and endeavour to make their pilgrimage at Knock as comfortable and as prayerful as possible. After a lot of discussion, we designed a uniform for them, entirely white, to symbolise the Apparition: a long white coat, its pocket embroidered with a rosary entwining the letters CM, meaning *Cumhal Mhuire*, Slave of Mary, and on the peak of the veil, a golden rose. The stewards would help to organise the processions and the crowds, as well as some aspects of the liturgy, and, of course, would provide for the general welfare of pilgrims, attending to wheelchairs, stretchers – very common then – and all manner of general organisation. The stewards would wear a navy blazer, grey slacks and a tie with the Apparition symbol.

We were starting from nothing and it was a difficult task to plan for such an organisation. In the end, we decided to invite the help of people who had a record of proven and acknowledged achievement, as it is a fact that people who have most to do are often the very people who will take on more. We had James and Bridie Morrin, business people from Kiltimagh, Bridie was to become secretary to the handmaids; Paddy Houlihan, manager of a local bank, and his wife, Kathleen, who singly and together gave invaluable help; Mrs Kate Mullaghy from Castlebar, who was Archbishop Gilmartin's sister; Dr Eibhlin Flannery, a medical doctor from Tubbercurry, who was for a time superintendent of the handmaids; and Tom Maguire from Dublin. Tom had organised some Dublin pilgrimages, in particular the big one in 1929, when we first took notice of Knock, and he was the most helpful man imaginable with excellent suggestions on so many matters.

Sometime during those fresh eventful years, I went one day to a sale of work which the Medical Missionaries of Mary, then a very new order, were holding in the Mansion House in Dublin, and there, quite by accident, I got talking to a woman who was looking after one of the stalls. I was interested in the goods she had on offer and after a little time, she introduced herself as Countess O'Byrne. Inevitably, I told her about Knock which, to me, was a wonderful story. She appeared to be very interested and, that evening, on my suggestion, she and her husband, Count Patrick, came round to our hotel where all four of us talked about the shrine for hours. They turned out to be a charming and most interesting couple, though it took a little time to learn their full story. They both belonged to very distinguished families who had very close links with some of the European aristocracy, and as a result, they had a great understanding of international affairs, of art, literature, music and religious matters.

They had taken an active part in the Independence movement, and in local affairs generally in north Tipperary. Then, in the very early days of the Free State, Patrick O'Byrne was sent to Italy, one of the first Irish diplomatic appointments. During their time in Rome, Countess Bernadette did a great deal of editorial work on the *Official Bulletin of Information*, which was published monthly and distributed among diplomatic circles in Rome and the Vatican. Inevitably, she had been hostess at numerous receptions, and arising from those years she had made several useful friends. She was a very kind woman, with a broad vision, who took me under her wing, so to speak, and saw to it that we were invited to meet almost everybody who could be useful to our work.

In due course, she took us both to meet the then papal nuncio, Dr Paschal Robinson at the Legation in the Phoenix Park. The submission of the Second Knock Commission of Enquiry was then about to go through his hands to Rome, but we knew that in the best diplomatic tradition, little would be said about it. However, I remember the nuncio, a tall man, who reminded me of a painting of one of the medieval saints. He asked me to come and sit by him, to tell him about Knock, and there we sat, on a red plush sofa, while he questioned me about facilities for confessions at the shrine, and whether pilgrims could get food there. It was interesting that he checked on the spiritual and physical needs of would-be pilgrims, though at the time, it seemed little more than small talk; he was a charming man and an excellent host. She also took us to meet Dr Douglas Hyde who had by then become the first president of Ireland. Long before that, Douglas Hyde had been recognised as a great Gaelic scholar and writer, so Liam, who was very familiar with his work, was delighted to meet him. They had plenty to talk about, and were never at a loss for words, though as well as talking about the Irish stories and Connaught love poems, we also spoke to him about Knock. The word ecumenism was not then commonly used, at least not in today's sense, and we must have been well ahead of our time that day, speaking about our Catholic shrine to our Protestant president. Douglas Hyde was, however, a Roscommon man, who knew and loved the west, a gentleman through and through, and he made us very welcome.

Very soon after that Countess O'Byrne became a handmaid, and in due course, because she was prepared to give sound advice, and follow up that advice with suitable action and hard work, she was made president of our Dublin sub-committee. For the rest of her life she made herself available to help with the normal work of the handmaids in whatever way she could. Before long we were able to open our first Dublin office, in a splendid position, South Anne Street, a prestigious focal point for the whole city, indeed it would have been difficult to find a better one. The Dublin handmaids, Countess O'Byrne and Maude and Evelyn Clarke, staffed it. The Clarkes lived in a large house, Laurel Hill, in Blackrock and taught music at one of the music colleges, but they gave their every free moment to Knock work. Very soon, we had Eileen O'Brien who had first class office skills, and Esther Ledwidge, who designed and made the most beautiful hats and had her own Dublin salon. Off and on in turn they all came to stay with us at Bridgemount, and in the long summer evenings we formulated plans and guidelines for the society, many of which are observed today.

From the beginning, it was understood that those handmaids and stewards would be moulded into a body of helpers whose personal lives would be of the highest moral standard. A very well-defined code of behaviour was and still is, laid down, and it has proved to be well worthwhile. Repeatedly, over the years, the devotion, self-effacement, courtesy and obvious caring of the handmaids and stewards have earned many favourable comments and letters from pilgrims who were seeing them for the first time. Visitors have always been deeply impressed by those voluntary helpers, but they could never be fully aware of the extent of their commitment. We, who are on the inside, knew that without that generous help and sheer dedication through the years, the development of the shrine as we know it today, might not have been achieved.

3

Publicity
Preparing first book
Radio Éireann talk
Gaiety Theatre lecture
First Knock Shrine *Annual*

One day while I was arranging flowers at the shrine, Canon Grealy came to me and without any preamble said, 'Tell Liam that I want him to write a book on Knock'. The canon was not normally a man to trifle unduly about things, but on that occasion, I laughed heartily at the idea as I honestly thought that he was joking and I said so. However, it soon became obvious that he was not at all in a trifling mood, and he meant every word that he was saying. I agreed to pass on the message, and as soon as I got home I told Liam about it. His reaction was more or less the same as mine had been, he too thought that the canon could not have been serious, so we forgot all about it. It turned out however that it was not all that easy to forget it, as each time we met the canon he asked how the book was getting on, and if it would soon be finished. Bit by bit we began to realise that there was no getting out of doing it, he fully expected it, and anyway, it was becoming pretty clear that perhaps sooner rather than later, it would have to be tackled. Writing a book was not then very high on the list of things to be done, but all of a sudden it had become urgent, and there was nothing to be done but get on with it.

Canon Grealy was a familiar figure at Knock at that time. He always wore his biretta and cape, and he could usually be found walking up and down outside the church with his hands behind his back saying his rosary. His two sprightly hounds, his close companions in all situations, Sheila and Ruby, trotted beside him. He was the soul of hospitality and he often invited people to call to his house of an afternoon to 'tea and pancakes', at which his housekeeper apparently excelled, and which he obviously enjoyed. He loved to go fishing, and whenever he had a few hours to spare and the weather was favourable, he would take himself off to fish on a small lake nearby.

At the time we first took an interest in Knock, Canon Grealy had had the inside of the church refurbished a short time before, and as well as that, he had placed three large plaster statues of the figures of the Apparition at the gable. It was clear from the beginning that, unlike so many of his brother priests, he was sympathetic and open to the whole question of the Apparition. He was not a young man then, and in the years that followed he must have had misgivings from time to time, seeing his relatively peaceful parish life disrupted by the things we were trying to achieve and which, in his eyes, must have had little to do with the work of his parish. No doubt, he questioned the wisdom of our actions now and then, but it must be emphasised, and emphasised again and again, that nothing was ever undertaken by us without his agreement and permission. Sometimes however, his reaction when those things were finally carried out was another story.

With the experience of years, it is somewhat easier to recognise the difficulties and appreciate the problems we must have caused, not just for Canon Grealy, but for parish priest after parish priest. The moment he was appointed to his parish, there we were, eternally asking for permissions for this and that, inevitably things which, if granted, would generate an increased workload such as extra confessions and the many other demands of pilgrims, when the resources to carry out those extra tasks did not exist. One can appreciate such problems at this distance, but in youth, when very involved, committed and enthusiastic, one was not always so philosophical. Many times over the years, when plans for some forthcoming special event had been carefully thought out, discussed and agreed upon, with all the arrangements made to carry them through, it was extremely difficult and frustrating to find them being suddenly resisted, often at the eleventh hour. To make things even more difficult, those plans had always been discussed with the archbishop and carried his full permission. However, we do not live in a perfect world, and it must be a credit to all concerned that the whole story of the development of Knock has been free from any serious disagreement. No matter how difficult the negotiations might have been, somehow they were always resolved diplomatically in the end, though without doubt that was due entirely to the grace of God working within all of us.

After a great deal of thought and deliberation, Liam decided to make a start with the book. It was not an easy task. The one or two books about the Apparition which had been published years before were long out of print, and in any event, after more than fifty years, the evidence needed fresh evaluation. Interest in Knock had been very keen and widespread at the time the Apparition had taken place, with both British and Irish papers reporting on it in detail. Contemporary newspapers and their reports were therefore the most valuable source of information, and that meant several journeys to the National Library in Dublin, where exhaustive searches had to be made into old files. I understand that it is possible to consult old papers very easily and quickly on microfilm today, but it was not so in the 1930s.

Seeking out the relevant years and dates and taking care not to miss any others that might not already have been checked meant that it was a very time-consuming task, and most tedious. Numerous journeys were required to complete the work, which, bearing in mind the distance involved, meant a lot of driving. It is difficult to realise now that even the so-called main roads were then absolutely dreadful, being little more than narrow, winding dust roads with more than their share of potholes; so a journey to Dublin could take several hours. The cars were also basic: they had no heaters, ventilators, screen washers or any of the facilities taken for granted today; their springing was also somewhat crude and often got broken, giving a bumpy ride, and flat tyres were commonplace. All in all, a long journey could prove to be an endurance test, even with a new car.

Little or no systematic research had been carried out on the history of Knock since the time of the Apparition, nor had any effort been made to keep it up to date, but bit by bit all available reports and source material were examined afresh and all the information was collected and collated.

We were fortunate also that two witnesses to the Apparition were still alive, Pat Byrne and Mrs Mary O'Connell. Pat Byrne was only a boy in 1879, but Mrs O'Connell was in her late twenties at the time. When we met her, she had a vivid recollection of every detail of that night, and when we told her that we were preparing a book about it with the authority of Canon Grealy and the archbishop, she offered to give us every possible help. During all of our questioning, which must have been very tedious to her as she was no longer a young woman, we found her most co-operative and helpful. She never spoke about the Apparition to anybody unless requested to do so; indeed we often marvelled at her gentle manners and patience with the large numbers of pilgrims who came to her house at all hours of the day and even into the night looking for information. During those months, she told us many things and elaborated on details which, in the years that followed, proved to be of great significance.

There were also many others still living who had clear memories of that night and were happy to tell us about it. There was Margaret Hartigan of the Royal George Hotel, Limerick, whose parents had owned a large farm on the Limerick-Cork border shortly after the Apparition. She clearly remembered as a child seeing pilgrims en route to Knock from the south, travelling in large numbers on foot, some of them sleeping in outhouses at their farm, and seeing them again days later on their return journey. Some people in the adjoining towns, Ballyhaunis and Kiltimagh, could remember the vigils of 15 August when the pilgrim traffic with its horses, donkeys and carts, kept them awake at night. Then there were those who were claiming cures, and they were wonderful to listen to with their profound gratitude and total sincerity. Such was the strength of faith in those days that most of them regarded those cures almost as a natural development.

Meantime, I seemed to be driving all over Connaught following up reports of other cures, reports which were at best sketchy, and all too often, inaccurate. It cannot be stressed too frequently that some people did not take Knock seriously then, and they often dismissed the question of re-ported cures with scorn. In my desk, I still have a slim note-book into which I pencilled details of my first searches. Since the first listing of cures by Archdeacon Cavanagh, around forty years before, very little had been checked thoroughly or verified, and much of the so-called 'information' was little more than rumour and was therefore useless. We were faced with compiling this book, and one had to be extra careful checking and re-checking for accuracy.

I remember setting out on my first journey looking for some concrete facts. It is all as clear as if it had happened only yesterday, as I can still sense the almost perceptible disbelief among people I went to talk to. It was as if they could not accept that a mature, and apparently rational young woman, could be talking about such foolish things. Liam had gone to a court that morning, and as he was very busy officially at the time, and there was a great deal still to be done with the book, I set out alone. It was Ash Wednesday, a cold dry day in March with pale hazy sunshine. I was driving a small Austin car at the time, it was one of the first of the small cars, and I was very happy with it. After my customary silent prayer, I sat in and drove out through the gates at the end of the avenue. I was full of high hopes and expectations, but as I went up a hill near the house, a large section of a very high stone wall fell on to the road just a couple of feet ahead of me. There was no time to stop, so I drove on, it seemed almost through, the stones, which were falling around me. It was a frightening experience, which I have never forgotten. How I escaped, and without a scratch on myself or on the car, I do not know, but I was pretty shaken when I stopped and saw the large pile of stones which had fallen behind me almost blocking the road. However, after a few minutes' consideration, I realised that I had not been hurt, there didn't appear to be any damage done to the car, and I saw no reason to abandon my trip, so I continued on my journey.

Canon Grealy had told me about a boy who had been cured a few years before. He lived, I understood, near Kiltimagh, and had gone to school there, so, with the name of the village, the school and the name of his teacher, which should have been quite enough, I set out to find him. I called at the school and found the teacher, but he had never heard of the boy or of the cure. However, he was very polite and didn't laugh at my enquiry, at least not to my face. He suggested other people who might be of help, but though I sought each one out and found them, some I should add whose response was very amusing, at least amusing in retrospect, none could offer any assistance. After several hours driving and talking with every suggested likely lead, I decided that the whole thing was merely one more rumour without any foundation. Tired, disillusioned and very, very hungry, for it was then late afternoon, I knew that I had had enough. However, something prompted me to make just one other call, and that was on Mrs Bridie Morrin.

I had met Mrs Morrin on a train returning from Dublin a little time before. As one often did on a long journey in those days, I got into conversation with her, and spoke to her about Knock. Like so many others, she was very sceptical about the whole thing at first, but as she listened to me she became interested. Before we parted company at Claremorris where the train divided, one bit going to Westport, the other to Kiltimagh and beyond, she asked me to call on her when next in Kiltimagh, if I had time, and we could talk again. It seemed an unlikely possibility at the time, but now how glad I was to remember that offer, and to see if I could enlist her assistance. Mrs Morrin had been a worker at Lourdes for over thirty years at the time, and had received their Silver Medal, though I didn't know about that for several years afterwards. Her husband, James, was a businessman and they lived in a large house, St Mary's, at the edge of the town. In the years that followed, Bridie and James Morrin gave devoted service to Knock and became wonderful friends, often giving vital encouragement in difficult situations.

At once she offered to come with me to find the boy, as she too was perplexed that in the course of my enquiries, two villages, one north, the other south, had been mentioned to me as the most likely places to find him. So before we set out she suggested that we should say a prayer to the Holy Souls to help us to pick the right one. Mrs Morrin was a deeply spiritual person who, since the time she was a boarder in The Bower, Athlone, had a great devotion to the Holy Souls, and she had made what she called the Heroic Offering, which was offering all her prayers and works for them. I prayed with her that afternoon for the souls of the departed, and we then decided on the village to approach. Ever since that day, I have always prayed to the Holy Souls before beginning anything of importance, and I must admit they have never failed me. As soon as we had finished our few prayers, we drove off in the direction of the village.

A mile or so along the road we met a girl cycling towards us. Mrs Morrin, recognising her, asked me to pull up and, letting down the window of the car, she spoke to her. Our Lady of Knock or the Holy Souls must have been guiding us, for after all the fruitless searches and disappointments of the morning, the girl turned out to be the teacher's sister and she knew all about the boy who was reported to have been cured. She said that it was difficult to find his house, and without a moment's hesitation she offered to come with us to show us the way, pushing her bicycle behind a hedge as she spoke – an offer which, needless to say, was accepted very quickly. She got into the car and I drove on. Then, after a mile or two, she asked me to stop, and she said that we would have to walk from there as the boreen was unsuitable for cars from that point. We left the car and began to walk. After a couple of minutes we saw a boy coming towards us walking on stepping stones across a small stream and carrying a can. We hardly noticed him at first as he appeared to be like any other boy, but our guide told us that this was the lad we were looking for, and calling him by his name, 'John', she asked him if his mother was at home. On hearing that she was in, I asked the girl if she would go into the house, a thatched cottage, and ask the mother to come and talk to us, which she did without any hesitation.

The boy's mother was a woman probably in her forties. She came out at once, and seemed to be not at all surprised that we had come. We asked her to tell us about the boy, and she told us all that we had come to hear. As she spoke to us tears streamed freely down her face, and it was obvious that she was deeply moved. The child had never walked until she had taken him to Knock several years before. They were very poor and like so many people in the west then, her husband had to go to England to find work, so responsibility for running the small farm, caring for a crippled child, together with her other children, as well as for a blind father-in-law, seemed to have been her painful lot. From the moment she had realised that the child could not walk at the usual age, that his feet and legs were becoming deformed and bent underneath him, and that the small amount of medical aid she had sought had done little to help, she had, she told us, had a firm belief that if she could take him to Knock for the Vigil on the eve of 15 August, Feast of the Assumption, he would be cured. Accordingly, on 14 August a few years before she had set out carrying the child on her shoulders, a journey probably of about fourteen miles. Once arrived at the shrine, she completed the traditional stations and the full vigil, walking home again in the morning still fasting, but there was no change in John's condition. The following year she set out again, and again returned home with the child still unable to walk, but this time with the added trial of having to listen to her father-in-law's taunts about her folly.

Another year passed and undeterred, on 14 August she set out for Knock again. By that time, the boy was over five years old, and a considerable weight to carry. Neighbours who were also going on pilgrimage that night offered her a lift in a farm cart but she declined, reasoning to herself that no cure would be granted to her without prayer and a great deal of penance. For the third year, she completed her long and increasingly tiresome walk and, having arrived at Knock, she began the Stations of the Cross. At the third station, John, who could talk plenty, called out to her, 'Mother, Mother, let me down, I want to walk!' At once, she put him down and to her delight, he was able to stand; the deformed feet had become straight, and he could walk for the first time. He walked with her inside the church and then outside the church, he walked to show the other pilgrims that he could walk, he walked to complete the night's devotions, a very big walk for a very small boy. Subsequently his condition improved rapidly and in due course his case was examined and reported on favourably by his doctor. Then, following a promise made that night to Our Lady, John and his mother walked to Knock on 14 August every year for a vigil of prayer and thanksgiving. Years later, when he was fully-grown, he worked on the land in full health.

John was not the only one we found, as news of our work spread. People came to tell us about wonderful cures and favours, a rapidly developing pattern which made it quite clear in our minds that they had just been waiting for such a moment to tell someone. Bit by bit facts were put together and the book took shape, the full account of the Apparition: to the best of our ability reports of cures and the history of the shrine within the fifty years that had just ended, bringing the whole history up to date. At length, the manuscript was completed, ecclesiastical approval given and the first copies of the book, *Knock Shrine*, were delivered to us from the printer on the Feast of the Miraculous Medal, 27 November 1935.

We wasted no time in taking a copy to Canon Grealy, who was delighted with it, and when he had read it he wrote a very gracious letter of praise to Liam. We made an appointment to see the archbishop and as we drove to Tuam that misty November day and called on him, we wondered yet again how we might be received. We were shown into his study and he came to us at once. He greeted us warmly, though we knew him only slightly at the time, and without any delay or formality, we gave him the book. I shall never forget his face when he received his copy. He remained standing in his study though he had asked us to sit, he took the book in his hands and went slowly to the bow window to get better light, and then he began to read. After a very, very long time, reading and turning the pages slowly, he suddenly remembered that we were still there in the room waiting for him and he was full of apologies. He said that he was delighted with his first impressions of the book, and he looked forward to reading it. He also said that he felt it would do a great deal of good. *Knock Shrine* was well reviewed in the papers and journals and ran to several editions. It created a fresh interest in the shrine as a completely new generation including our own could read a complete account of the Apparition for the first time.

We were by then very concerned about trying to get the right type of publicity for the shrine. It was essential to highlight the exact details of the Apparition as they had been reported, and to make an uninformed public aware of its richness and magnitude. Despite the fact that an official commission of enquiry had taken evidence from witnesses within six weeks of the event and while memories of the night were clear and vivid, accurate accounts had, by the 1930s, become almost impossible to find. In 1935, few people realised that anything other than a vision of the Blessed Virgin had been seen at Knock. While Archdeacon Cavanagh was parish priest, reported miracles were very frequent and pilgrims thronged there daily. Over the years, however, interest had waned somewhat, except on the two Marian feasts, 15 August and 8 September, and on the days between, when country people always came on pilgrimage because it was harvest time, the culmination of the farming year and it was time to give thanks and pray. However, because of occasional discouragement from the clergy, and above all else, because no official steps had been taken to state otherwise, inevitably reports about the whole event had become trivialised. Nothing of much consequence had happened there since the initial interest at the time of the Apparition, certainly since the time of Archdeacon Cavanagh's death, until that day when Tom Maguire of Dublin organised a large pilgrimage of the St Vincent de Paul Society from St Michan's Parish, Dublin city, and Fr Tuffy, then parish priest, invited the archbishop, Dr Gilmartin, to speak. That, in fact was the beginning of the revival of Knock.

We approached Radio Éireann, as it then was, to ask if they would consider broadcasting a feature on the shrine. After some time, when we had almost decided that they had forgotten about it, they came back to us to say that as Liam had done all the research, and as far as they could make out, knew more about the subject than anybody else around at the time, he should consider doing a broadcast talk himself, and they would make all facilities available to him. After much thought and, as usual, prayer, he finally decided that he should do so, and a date was fixed. The plan was that he would do a fifteen-minute talk, which was quite a long time on such a sensitive subject, but as it turned out, that much time was necessary to cover it in reasonable depth.

There were no local radio stations then, so on the appointed day we set out for Dublin and our first encounter with radio. Dr T. J. Kiernan was director of broadcasting; his wife, Delia Murphy, then a very popular ballad singer who was being heard regularly on the radio and on records, came into the old studios in Henry Street to meet us. Having come from Mayo herself, she had heard that some Mayo people were coming to broadcast, and with characteristic concern, she had decided to call in to make us feel more at home, even though we didn't know each other. She was wonderfully kind and thoughtful, sitting with me during the transmission to put me at ease while I listened, a gesture that helped me greatly, as when the time came I was very nervous and hardly recognised Liam when the broadcast began. I truly thought it was somebody else, but I have since learned that that is a common first-hearing reaction. There was no pre-recording in those days, everything went out live, which was a bit of an ordeal. Delia had a very keen sense of humour which put people at ease at once and she was a great help to me that day. She was very interested in the Mayo shrine which, like all of us, she remembered from childhood. Very soon after that broadcast we were approached by somebody who had a very significant contribution to make towards our development, and who, quite by accident, was among the listeners that day.

One day a short time afterwards we were returning from a meeting in Dublin and got on to a train at Westland Row, carrying papers and a couple of books, and looking forward to a quiet read *en route*. We were vaguely aware of a lone lady who sat in the corner of our carriage, intently reading the *Irish Times* and paying no attention whatever to anybody else. One glance was enough to tell her background, her well-cut tweeds, sensible shoes, felt hat and general appearance said it all, she was 'county' when 'county' was indeed a fact of life to be reckoned with. Minutes before the train was due to leave, along came Delia running in search of a seat and, recognising us, she came at once to join us. Without wasting too much time on formalities, she began to chat and to tell some hilarious stories, which she had in abundance. She was a natural comedian with a very

58

infectious hearty laugh, and she took no notice whatever of the other occupant of the carriage. Long before the train had cleared the city boundaries, the 'Irish Times' in the corner began to shake and the reader was rocking with laughter. In no time at all she too was joining in the fun and enjoying herself immensely. Such was Delia's gift for breaking down barriers. Had she not joined us, we would probably have read our papers and books all the way home, and it would have been just a routine journey. The tweedy lady turned out to be a member of a well-known Mayo family, who certainly enjoyed that memorable trip home from town. After that, we all remained in touch for many years.

Video recording had not then been dreamed of, but sometime around that time Dr Jack Lyons, the medical doctor in Kilkelly, who was a keen amateur photographer, came to us and offered to make a movie film on Knock. We were delighted at the kind offer, as a movie film was a very advanced resource at the time, with possibly only one or two such cameras in the whole county, perhaps the province. Then, following comprehensive planning and discussion, he came over to Knock Sunday after Sunday to record the pilgrimages on 16mm film. He went to Claremorris to meet the pilgrimage trains and film everything relevant at the time. He then took on the task of editing and spent hours working on it at his home, a house which still stands, high on a hill outside Kilkelly on the way to Knock airport. In due course, a very interesting documentary film was put together. I have it still, with all its views of the old Knock, striking images of the stark conditions of the times, and in sharp contrast with the amenities now available to pilgrims. Of particular interest are some sequences of shots of Mrs O'Connell who came with me one evening that summer to the first candlelight procession. She was particularly delighted that the processions had been restored as, before that, they had been dropped for several years. The film was a very useful piece of publicity as for the first time there was a visual record, as far as it was humanly possible to provide one, of everything that had happened, and was continuing to happen at the shrine.

The moment it was ready, we set up a lecture tour covering the whole country. It was organised carefully and thoroughly. Paddy Houlihan, a banking friend and a steward, came with us and dealt with the projection and generally with the technical side. It was, of course, a silent film, there were no facilities then for dubbing a soundtrack with either commentary or music, so Liam did the commentary live, and answered questions afterwards. If the weather was particularly bad Pat Burke came too, as the problem of the journey home on a winter night was always at the back of our minds, and in such circumstances, the more of us there were, the better. The film was screened in cinemas, halls and other meeting places according as people showed an interest. We would drive back to Bridgemount, very late at night, usually in the small hours, often after a long long journey, tired to exhaustion point and glad to sink into the safety and comfort of home.

One night we took the film to Maynooth College, at that time solely a sanctuary for the clergy and their students and they had a formidable audience of clerics, students and dignitaries assembled to greet us. Monsignor Dalton, afterwards cardinal, who was then president of the college, invited us, but in truth, the invitation was organised on the suggestion of Fr Jarlath Ronayne from Roscrea, an old friend of his, and whom we had met at Knock a short time before when he came there to preach. It was heartening to hear Monsignor Dalton's warm welcome, as we were not at all sure in advance as to how we might be received in that bastion of clerical rectitude, but in fairness to all of them, they gave us a tremendous reception. Over the years since then, several priests have come to me in Knock and told me that they first heard about the shrine that evening in Maynooth when they were students.

As we drove home that night, through a raging gale which forced us to drive in low gear almost all the way, we talked enthusiastically about their response. We felt for the first time that we were beginning to make an impact and were breaking through some of the prejudice. To do so on that level seemed to be a tremendous achievement, though in honesty, their minds were probably more receptive and sympathetic than those of the men who were directly concerned. For that successful venture we were indeed very grateful to God. During that season, we also took the film to the monastery in Roscrea, the permission for such a visit being then a very great privilege, and, to round off, we went to a few venues in Belfast.

Later that year we decided to take the Gaiety Theatre in Dublin, and arrange a Sunday public symposium on Knock shrine. It was important to organise it in Dublin, the capital city, where we knew we could count on maximum audience and publicity. I don't remember which of us thought up the idea first, but once decided upon, there was no stopping us. Taking a theatre anywhere is a big venture at any time, but the idea of taking Dublin's most prestigious theatre for such a purpose sounded ambitious by any standards, foolhardy by most. Somebody suggested that to make the venture more attractive we should have musical interludes between the speakers, and that we should invite the then budding Dublin Operatic Society to come and sing some appropriate music. Unaware of, and equally unconcerned about the calibre of the Dublin Operatic, I wrote to their director, and was not one bit surprised when he replied saying that they would be pleased to sing. By my reckoning, if I had reckoned on that aspect of the operation at all, they, and not Knock, would be the recipients of any honour going that day and indeed they came, they sang and they were most impressive. The film was the centrepiece of the occasion, with Liam, as usual, doing the commentary. Guest speakers that day included the Minister for Education, Tomás Ó Deirg, and Dr G. Tierney of Dublin, while Dr George Maguire of Claremorris was in the chair. We had a full house, and as Radio Éireann broadcast the whole programme, news of the shrine was spreading rapidly.

During the following year, it was decided that as the pilgrimages were beginning to grow in number, a record of them, and indeed of everything relevant to the growth and development of the shrine, should be kept. By that time we had begun to keep a diary of pilgrimages, not many it is true in those days, but they were growing steadily. With that for basis, the first *Knock Shrine Annual* came into being. An editorial told of all new developments, small things by today's standards, but momentous then, and each one a milestone along the road. Beneath each apparently small story, there frequently lay a saga of great endeavour. There were a few photographs; some articles specially written for us; a list of our promoters, or people who were helping us with their prayers and their pennies and were generally trying to make the shrine better known; a list of all those who had given gifts of any kind; a list of 'Favours Received' which included, as far as we were allowed to publish them, reports of cures; a financial statement; and an obituary column. The first *Annual* was published in March 1938 and it was well received. Its publication has continued, thanks to the generosity of numerous contributors through the years, as a voluntary effort. Nobody other than the printer is paid and the *Annual* is sold at a price which just about covers costs. A full file of bound copies has been kept, and there is one in the

National Library. It is the only complete record of everything that has happened at Knock since the foundation of the society and through it, researchers in future years will be able to find precise information and dates when required.

Today, when national and indeed international radio can cover an event in seconds, and magnificent live television pictures bring a story into the home at the touch of a switch, it is difficult to imagine a time when the local and national papers sent a reporter, who took extracts from the homily in shorthand, and at the end, would telephone his office on the old wind-up telephone, giving details of it and any other newsworthy event, and one read of it next day or maybe next week. I suppose it was small wonder if those reporters might at times have overstretched the imagination, no doubt a sensational story was important even then! I can still sense the excitement of the days when the Radio Éireann engineers would arrive at Knock for a broadcast of some special event on the day before the transmission, and the special choir, which had been rehearsed for months, came in early for a microphone 'balance test'. We were all at fever pitch as they tested telephone links and the other bits of 'high tech' which they had brought with them. It was a great moment when Knock came 'on the air' and, for an hour or two we were at the centre of things, with our very own broadcast to the whole country, telling them about Our Lady's shrine down in the west.

In those days if somebody could somehow have looked into the future and given us a hint of the development of that shrine in the lifetime of even some of us, we would have dismissed it as a flight of fancy. All of that, however, was still a long, long way off. A great deal of work awaited us and many others before that dream could be realised.

4

Lourdes pilgrimage 1935
Conditions in Knock
PTAA Pilgrimage

I t is, I suppose in the nature of things that one remembers the early days of all experience, and the early days for us at Knock were certainly memorable. Perhaps it was because everything was so new to us, and the character of the work so different from any other we had known. I have always had, and thank God I continue to have, a very good memory, so images from those years remain as clear as if they were only from yesterday. We were still very new to things in the mid 1930s, and alongside all the successes, there were always the disappointments and the difficulties, trivial, I suppose when looked at now, yet of great importance to us at the time.

In September 1935, Liam and I went to Lourdes again, this time with a large Franciscan pilgrimage, which, long before the days of planes and mass travel, was going by liner from Dublin. It was a big event for all concerned, and we looked forward to it with great pleasure. By then, we had done a considerable amount of research into the whole subject of Knock; the book, *Knock Shrine*, was in final proof, just before publication and naturally, we had our prayer leaflet with us, so we were reasonably well prepared and generally satisfied with progress. Travelling with us was Liam's sister, Mother Genevieve, from the Convent of Mercy in Westport. She was very good company and also a great nun, deeply spiritual, yet very practical and full of good sense. Mrs Bridie Morrin was also travelling; by that time we had got to know her well, and she in turn had become well versed in Knock affairs. She had been a regular helper at Lourdes for years, so she knew her way about there and had a thorough knowledge of all the routines of the place, a knowledge that turned out to be a help to all of us.

Almost as soon as we had arrived, she suggested to me that I should go to her hotel one evening to talk about Knock to the group who were staying there. In those days I was delighted to get an opportunity to talk about Knock to anybody, so I readily agreed. Having been given the all clear by me she went ahead and made the arrangements, so after dinner one night she came along to escort me, and I went with her, not giving the matter a second thought. I have never been nervous about talking to people, and in the years that followed it was something I had to do very often. On arrival at her hotel though, I was a little taken aback to discover that Mrs Morrin had assembled what seemed a huge number of people in a very large room, and there they all sat waiting to hear what I had to say. They were mostly some of the Irish pilgrims who had travelled out with us, but I was surprised when I was told that Dr Mageean, bishop of Down and Connor, who was also staying at that hotel, would be in the audience. I had little time to consider the matter however, as, almost as soon as I entered the room I was introduced to him. He appeared to be a very pleasant sort of man, but a bishop! I had never had a bishop in my audience before and I wondered briefly how he might react to my talk. Fortunately, I had little or no time to dwell on it. I had some of our prayer leaflets in my bag and, opening it, I handed him one, while I put some more on the table in front of us, so that anybody could take one if they felt so inclined.

At that point, a Franciscan priest who was standing behind Dr Mageean's chair, leaned over, took one of the leaflets in his hand, turned it over and studied it for a moment, then, looking at me with visible disdain, he said to the bishop in a loud voice for all to hear, 'Oh! My Lord, this leaflet has only got *Cum permissu superiorum.*' – a permission which is considerably less impressive than the more authoritative *Imprimatur*, and he paused to consider the effect his pronouncement was having on the assembled company. At the same time, he kept his eye fixed firmly on me to witness no doubt with pleasure, my inevitable put down. Holding my breath I waited while the bishop took the leaflet in his hand, examined it very, very carefully and glanced at the back. He then turned to the priest, and said with a smile and in an equally loud voice, 'Father, Dr Gilmartin's *Permissu superiorum* is good enough for me', and nodding in my direction said very graciously, 'Please tell us about Knock, Mrs Coyne'. It was a small thing, but it showed how the wind was blowing at the time. The priest's derisory attitude was by then nothing new to us, and one we were to experience again and again among some of the clergy during those early years.

The following summer the Catholic Truth Society held a congress in Tuam, ending with a garden party which was to be held in the grounds of the cathedral on the closing day. *Knock Shrine* had by then been published, and we asked the archbishop if he would allow us, the society, to erect a tent in the grounds where we could tell people about the shrine, distribute leaflets and answer questions about it – probably for the first time – correctly. It seemed to us to be an ideal opportunity to publicise devotion to Knock, one that we felt should not be missed. He gave permission readily enough and he asked Canon Joe Walsh, who was at that time president of St Jarlath's College, and was later to become archbishop, to arrange a position for us somewhere within the cathedral grounds. Canon Walsh, who had a great sense of humour, got enormous fun for some reason out of the idea of us in a tent. Still, in fairness to him, he found us a spot, a splendid one as it turned out, almost in front of the cathedral door, under a tree which, I am sad to say, is no longer there.

We had not then reached designing uniforms for hand-maids and a few of us were on duty – I clearly remember long chiffon dresses and very large picture hats – so, dressed to kill in best garden party attire, we positioned ourselves as directed. As part of the programme there was a procession of bishops, which probably included most of the bishops of Ireland. In those days, such processions were a great array of colour and splendour, with all the bishops wearing long purple capes, some, probably archbishops, with flowing trains, surplices richly trimmed with lace and shoes with silver buckles. As we watched the impressive pageant with its almost medieval magnificence return slowly to the cathedral, a lone figure detached itself and came towards us. It was Dr Mageean, who had seen our tent in passing and, re-membering the incident at Lourdes the year before, had deliberately come to talk to us and enquire about the pro-gress of the society. He understood very well the problems we were trying to deal with and he wanted to show his sup-port for us, and let everybody who cared to look, see that he was giving it.

Also on that 1935 pilgrimage to Lourdes, we met a Miss Brigid Gleeson who came from Killarney. She was a great talker, and it didn't take us very long to discover that she was a committed nationalist, who loved all things Irish, and was a devoted follower of the whole Irish movement. Inevitably, we got talking about Knock, and as it was an Irish shrine, she naturally felt that it should be helped in every possible way. She was also very definite in her opinion that if properly developed, it would be a great boon to the

Irish people. One evening, during one of her many conversations with us, when she was considering the various avenues we might usefully explore, she said out of a thought that she had a nephew who was a monsignor in Rome, and she suggested that we should meet him when he next came to Ireland. The idea of getting to know somebody who was well placed in Rome sounded most attractive to us then, with the evidence from the Second Commission of Enquiry about to be taken up and sent there, so we agreed very readily. We were not aware at that stage however, of the calibre of the 'nephew in Rome', for he turned out to be none other than the legendary Monsignor O'Flaherty. In 1935, he had not yet embarked on the daring exploits which, during the Second World War, turned him into a legend, but we were soon to discover that the character on which it was eventually built was already quite remarkable.

Some time after our return home, we had a telegram one morning from Miss Gleeson informing us that Monsignor O'Flaherty would be in Knock the following day and would be seeking us out. I am certain that she had organised him to come there so that he might be able to help us in some way. Next day we went over to Knock and met him, and I remember he spent a long time talking to us. As it happened to be 8 September, there were large numbers of pilgrims present, not in organised pilgrimages, but in family groups who were walking slowly round the old church and quietly praying. He asked us about the organisation of that particular day, and when we told him that nobody had organised it, as on special feast days like it and 15 August, people had always come of their own accord, he was greatly impressed. He asked us about various aspects of the devotions and, in particular, about the facilities available to pilgrims for confession, facilities which he considered to be of the greatest importance, and which at that time were, of necessity, minimal.

He then spoke about the Commission of Enquiry which had just begun at the time, and he suggested that as an extra measure, we should get signatures from people of consequence in as many sections of society and regions of the country as possible, and send those signatures to Rome in the form of a petition for the shrine's recognition. Since Monsignor O'Flaherty was then a very high-ranking official within the Holy Office, it was reasonable to believe that he was well briefed in ecclesiastical protocol. In due course, we discussed the monsignor's conversation and advice with the canon and with the archbishop and, following on from that, we took on the task of collecting signatures.

Before he left us, Monsignor O'Flaherty told us that he would be delighted to help us in Rome on any matter and at any time, and if in the future we might need that help, he asked us not to hesitate to contact him. The war came and went, and it was another decade before we had to seek the aid of the monsignor, who, by that time had become a very celebrated man indeed, not just in Rome, as his fame had then spread across the whole of Europe. However, we sought him out, and true to his promise, he helped us through a difficult situation.

By the late 1930s, we had a book, we had a society, we had a medical bureau and we had some splendid handmaids and stewards, but at Knock, conditions were very difficult. For those who approach the shrine today, be it through the Claremorris or Kiltimagh gates, it would be impossible to visualise how it looked in the 1930s. Today, to the right and left of the drives, lush green lawns charm the eye, a luxuriance of flowers and shrubs, an ornamental lake and, crowning the panorama, the large white Basilica. One would have to make a wide search to discover a more delightful pilgrim close. In the 1930s, on the gable side of the old church, or the Church of the Apparition, as it is now called, a boundary wall ran almost beside the present lower gate, a few yards from the shrine, and beside it, a narrow dusty lane ran to what was then Byrne's pub, which stood almost on the site of the Basilica. There was no such thing then as a processional square, merely open fields.

Several times after the Apparition, the gable was stripped of its plaster by pilgrims who sought the old cement, as it was widely believed that many of the early cures came about through its application. In Archdeacon Cavanagh's day, not content with stripping the plaster, pilgrims began to take large stones from the wall, leaving gaping holes; no doubt were it left unattended, the whole gable would have been taken away. Twice, different parish priests had it replastered, but almost as quickly it was stripped again. In the end, iron railings enclosed the entire area. Inside them, a couple of priests had been buried, and later, plaster statues representing the Apparition, were placed there by Canon Grealy. On the west side of the church, the main road ran as it still does, but it is hoped that in time, it will be rerouted, so that there can be an end to main road through traffic, and a quiet sanctuary may develop around the gable. To the east of the church, the present Calvary was then fairly new, but around it there was nothing, a rough stone wall was its perimeter. The Stations of the Cross were erected by the Knock Shrine Society almost at the beginning, but there was still little comfort and few amenities for pilgrims. Beyond this small and poor enclosure, barren stony hillocks faded into the distance. It was not a vista to gladden the heart.

In the very early days, we were allowed by the canon to erect a small hut facing the gable, and a little later, one facing the church door. One or two people may still remember those huts, they were the focal point of much of our early work. There was room inside the first one for one handmaid only, and there she sat, answering enquiries all through her hours of duty. That handmaid was frequently Mrs Houlihan, or maybe my sister, Peg, willing helpers working in dreadful conditions. Later, we extended that accommodation some distance along the boundary wall facing the gable, though with an open front, and for a roof, corrugated iron sheeting, in plain language, it was a shed. Today such conditions would be unthinkable, nobody would accept them, and in fairness, they did belong to a time of almost complete deprivation, with few concessions to comfort for a large number of people.

However, it gave us a chance to give invalids a modicum of shelter from the weather, as well as a cup of tea, or soup and a sandwich during the interval between Mass and devotions. In those days, there was no such thing as evening Mass, so pilgrims came in the morning for Mass and stayed on for devotions in the afternoon. The invalids were placed before the shrine for devotions, their only covering then being a selection of makeshift waterproof sheets and later, portable hoods made from some waterproof material. It was even before the days of plastic, which came much later. The hoods were little beehive shaped tents with metal supports, and the stewards pulled them into position covering the assembled sick in an effort to protect them from the wind and the rain. One by one, some other 'temporary' huts were erected, but until the Basilica was built, exactly forty-one years from the year we began, there was little any of us could have done to ease conditions for the sick in bad weather.

On days of very large pilgrimages, Mass was celebrated on the east wall of the church, where we erected a basic canvas tent to cover the portable altar and the celebrant. Pews were taken out of the church and placed on the grass for invalids, though permission to do so was always a tricky piece of negotiation. Then we had wooden stands made to

71

hold the stretchers, and raise them above the wet ground. Stretchers were very numerous in those days when, I suppose, there was a different school of thought about hospital treatment. However, despite our tents and our efforts, if the wind blew from the east there were problems, altar candles were blown out and altar cloths flapped in the breeze, while in general, the pilgrims endured a great deal of hardship. There was no question whatever of being able to sit for any part of the devotions and that often entailed a very long stand.

It was not until the first fully-enclosed shrine altar was erected by the Knock Shrine Society in 1940 that it was possible to have either Mass or devotions with any degree of protection and respect for the Host and comfort for the celebrants, but even that was minimal. It still left the pilgrims and the helpers at the mercy of the elements, and all too often they were drenched and had to face the homeward journey in that state. In later years when pilgrimages had grown to be very big, another outdoor altar was erected close to the shrine so that people could see it properly and follow the Mass. However, only the few priests who were officiating could be accommodated, while the dozens of others present had to stay with the procession, and there they stood to the end of Benediction, their long white vestments often soaked and clinging to their ankles, no doubt causing extreme misery for the wearers. It also presented enormous problems for the sacristan who was faced with the task of getting all those vestments dry again, with very poor facilities for doing so. Knock was truly a penitential pilgrimage for everybody in those days, but it did not deter the pilgrims, in fact the pilgrimages were immense.

By degrees, we negotiated with CIE to have special invalid coaches made for trains. They were the normal coaches adapted to carry stretchers and wheelchairs, but they made all the difference in handling the sick. The day before a pilgrimage, the Dublin handmaids, led by Eileen O'Brien worked through the day and a fair bit of the night, making sandwiches, soup and other food to give to the sick on the way to Knock and again on their return journey. Very early on the morning of their departure, the handmaids were on duty, meeting the invalids and helping to get them boarded, and they were on constant duty all the way to Knock. They were still on duty while they were there, and again on the return journey, so their day was equivalent to a normal two.

CIE, as they were then, ran numerous trains to the shrine in those days; we had 'invalid trains' and 'radio trains' and accommodation for the sick was relatively safe and comfortable in those specially designed coaches. From the moment of leaving the home station, the general body of pilgrims entered into the spirit of a pilgrimage with prayers and a suitable commentary relayed on loudspeakers through the train. One of the duties of the Knock handmaids and stewards was meeting the pilgrims' trains at Claremorris. This was not just a courtesy meeting carried out by a sort of hostess, there was plenty of hard work to be done there, as those trains frequently carried a large number of sick. In such situations, handmaids were always required, and stewards were needed for lifting and carrying, transferring patients from train to ambulance or bus and vice versa.

Some little time ago, one of our longer serving handmaids, Mrs Mary Gibbons, now alas, gone to her heavenly reward, told me that she remembers meeting as many as twenty-four trains on a 'busy day', and 'busy days' were then frequent. Mary Gibbons was then a very young handmaid, probably no more than a teenager, but she came to Knock every Sunday in the season, and in those days met every train as required. Pilgrims were taken to the shrine from the station while the sick travelled on specially adapted ambulance or bus. One loaded bus followed another, shunting along the winding dusty roads, smoking and spluttering as they lumbered up the hill to Knock. A memorable feature of those days also was the number of pilgrims who came on bicycles and on foot, often walking barefoot, and fasting. Some came in donkey carts, others in horse-drawn cars, horses were 'put up' somewhere in the village, while their owners prayed and maybe stopped afterwards to eat their few sandwiches. A few, very few, had cars. It was a situation in which anything might happen, yet everybody seemed to get safely home again.

It is almost impossible to believe that there was no main water supply in Knock in those days, a fact which made life very difficult for those of us who were endeavouring to work there. Every drop we used had to be brought from an old wheel-pump which stood close to the presbytery, though more often than not that pump was broken, and we had to go further afield for our supplies. It can be imagined what it was like trying to provide water for cooking or washing up, for even a modest number of people. The pump also supplied the residents of Knock and those who were making an effort then to feed the pilgrims. A few people in the village catered for pilgrims in those days, and St Mary's Hostel, which was then relatively new to Knock, also provided meals. Boiling kettles to get hot water, to wash up as well as to cook, must have been a nightmare for all of them. To give a meal to the helpers, apart at all from the invalids, was a major and carefully planned operation. A few primitive oil stoves stood in an equally primitive kitchen, and there we stood, trying to heat soup for the sick and boil water for tea; the meat and more solid food, I had already cooked and prepared at home. However, we could never, never, have enough water for washing up, so every drop was carefully measured. On warm days, when the low roofs of the huts warmed up, the all-pervading smell of the oil stoves mingling with the sickly smell of the tarred fabric on the roof was quite overpowering, yet one had to slog along and get on with it.

It took several years to get a main water supply, and even more important, that very basic requirement – public toilets. For years, pilgrims and helpers had to make do with field and dry toilets, inadequate by any standards and always a source of embarrassment to all of us who worked at the shrine. For years also there was no such thing as electricity or refrigeration, so things like electric kettles, carvers, blenders or even fridges were unknown. It was a constant nightmare endeavouring to keep perishables fresh, particularly in the sultry days of July and August, and we were then every bit as conscious of hygienic handling of food, perhaps even more so, than we are today, because of the problems we faced. If somebody had told us in those days about fridges, dishwashers, kettles or any other such appliances, we would have thought it too fantastic to be true; it was something we would never have expected to see in rural areas in our time.

It would be very difficult for the handmaids who now work in St John's, the invalids' building, where fridges, hot and cold water, modern cookers, adequate cutlery, dry tea-towels and reasonable seating are the norm, to imagine what conditions were like in those days. Sometimes as I watch them I wonder if perhaps the challenge which all of us, the first wave of handmaids had to face, inspired us to work with greater determination. There was the ever-present feeling of having to overcome some inevitable problem, it was almost a pioneering spirit which, in some peculiar way, brought out the best in all of us and united us solidly as we endeavoured to do everything as well as we possibly could. We were, of course, deeply conscious of the honour it was to be able to do that work for Our Lady and we did our utmost to do credit to her shrine. At the end of each day, there was the enormous satisfaction of knowing that we had done our best, and in sharing that feeling.

Some years later, when things should have begun to take shape at the shrine, the Pioneer Total Abstinence Association people approached us and said that they were planning a very big pilgrimage indeed for their members. From what they told us initially, it was obvious that it was going to be considerably bigger than anything we had handled to date, and we knew that we were facing a big challenge. However, delighted with the news and thrilled at the prospect, we went to tell the parish priest. All of this now seems almost incredible, even to me, when most pilgrimages are booked through the shrine office and dealt with in a rational manner by priests and staff. In those days, there was no such institution, and since we were the ones who then made all the arrangements, the organisers always approached us, the society, or more specifically me. We had several meetings to make sure that this particular pilgrimage would be organised perfectly, but it soon became obvious that, as far as the clergy were concerned, we were a nuisance. In the end, the only response we, and the Dublin members of the PTAA council got for our efforts, was an instruction to come to Knock, which we did.

There we were confronted with some of the civil authorities who had been specially requested to meet us and impress on us the futility of our plans. Mr Pierce Barrett, who was attached to the pioneers' pilgrimage, and some other members of his council, came from Dublin to talk about it, but they and we were made to listen to a catalogue of the tragedies that would befall us if we were to go ahead. 'The Mayo roads could not possibly take that sort of traffic', 'There would be no end of accidents and several people would be killed or maimed', 'We could never get enough guards to organise the traffic', and finally, as a comic etcetera, though the suggestion was made in all seriousness, 'We would have to get every tractor in Mayo to pull the cars out of the ditches'. It painted a heady picture of the pioneers' pilgrimage.

However, the pioneers had already made far too many arrangements to be put off: they had booked trains and buses, released a fair amount of publicity, and in general, laid several comprehensive and reasonable plans. Chief Superintendent O'Mara of the garda in Phoenix Park, was one of the main movers in the arrangements, as well as being chief marshal of the pilgrimage on the day, and we discussed with him well in advance all possible traffic problems. He had maps made of all approach roads to Knock, and when the day came, cars used one route to get there, another to leave. He organised a large garda presence to regulate traffic, in fact dozens of gardaí came to Knock the day before and spent the night in the old school. Sergeant O'Sullivan with his Knock gardaí made every possible effort to ensure that everything worked freely and without problems, as well as organising huge parking areas in nearby fields for the extra cars.

Between us, we called in the army who came along and dug trenches, then with what seemed to have been acres of canvas, they erected field toilets so that the thousands who were expected could be accommodated. In the end, thousands came, it was estimated about fifty, the biggest pilgrimage Knock had ever seen, in fact nothing like it was to be seen again until the Pope's visit, but it showed all of us what could be achieved. The day was a tremendous success with absolutely nothing left to chance, in fact, I would now venture to say that it was even more meticulously arranged than the papal visit, if that could ever be thought possible.

77

Once again it highlighted the difficulties under which we then worked, when every single plan we made, always with the enhancement of the shrine in mind, frequently met with outright opposition from those who should have been in there at least helping, if not themselves spearheading, such plans. There were several such days of intense frustration, when one wondered, and with good reason to wonder, where it might all end.

Despite all such setbacks, we coped. Nobody was aware that day of any tension, except for the very few close help-ers in whom we had confided, and everybody went home in the evening quite satisfied with everything. Of course, it is only fair to say that in those days, expectations generally were not high, and most people had to be content with very little. Nor must we lose sight of the fact that when our society was founded, the country was slowly emerging from decades of deprivation and even famine, which was still not far from living memory. The Land Wars, the Rising and the Civil War had passed away, but they had left their mark, and who could then have told about tomorrow. Neverthe-less, there was a wonderful atmosphere of hope, our ancient country was young again and we were all young together. A wonderful feeling of nationalism prevailed, people learned Irish, sang Irish songs and generally, we were proud of our country and were prepared to make the best of everything we had.

However, on the question of Knock, our national shrine, there were those people who for some strange reason, pre-ferred to look to the continent. France and Italy could offer shrines and devotions which were acceptable to them, but Knock, in their minds, despite the immensity and splendour of the Apparition, could never be viewed in the same light. There were those who gave splendid service to other shrines abroad, yet they had no interest in their own. This extraordinary attitude, which could have arisen only through ignorance of the facts about Knock, together with a pathetic immaturity and lack of self-confidence, remained until the time of the papal visit, when some, though by no means all of it, changed.

5

Dr Stafford Johnson
Medical Bureau
First recorded cure
Commission of Enquiry

V ery soon after the Radio Éireann talk on Knock in
1936, Liam received a letter one morning from a Dr
Stafford Johnson of Dublin, expressing great interest in the
talk, especially in the references that had been made to
cures. Dr Stafford Johnson was one of the leading ear, nose
and throat specialists in Ireland at the time; he was attached to some of the main hospitals in Dublin, and had his
consulting rooms in Fitzwilliam Square. As it happened, he
had heard the broadcast quite by chance. Until then he had
not known anything whatever about Knock and, as he was
a member of the medical bureau at Lourdes, a body which
examined all claims to cures there, he was interested to
know more about those mentioned in relation to Knock. A
lengthy correspondence followed, during which he asked us
if any similar arrangements had been made, or were being
planned at Knock. At that point, we had become very conscious of the difficulties that could arise if any claims to
cures arose and we were not in possession of all the facts
relating to each case, both before and after that claim. There
was also the problem of occasional inaccurate reporting of
cures which, if allowed to continue, could have done untold
harm to the shrine. Those were very real difficulties and almost from the beginning we had thought about the possibility of establishing some sort of body to deal specifically
with them, but while there were so many urgent things to

be done, such a foundation had, until that moment, seemed remote, so Dr Stafford Johnson's interest sounded providential.

On receipt of that letter, we went to see Canon Grealy and discussed it with him, and then on his suggestion, we wrote to the archbishop telling him about the enquiry and asking for his opinion. The archbishop's reply was immediate, in fact it came by return post, inviting Dr Stafford Johnson, Liam and myself to lunch at his house in Tuam to talk about it, on a date to be arranged between us. That seemed a logical progression and before long a date was fixed for the meeting. We then invited Dr Stafford Johnson to come to stay with us in Bridgemount, which he did, and he did so on several occasions afterwards. He was a tall, handsome man with a very keen sense of humour. Most of the people we dealt with in those days seem to have been blessed with that valuable quality. It was a very precious attribute as we came to realise over the years and there were many times when resorting to it was the only hope of dealing with some impossible situations.

In due course, we went to Tuam where we talked at great length with the archbishop about all the possible implications of the proposed medical bureau. I suppose the fact that Liam was a lawyer always prompted us to examine everything very thoroughly, and ensure that all aspects of any proposals that might have been under discussion were fully understood down to the last detail, not just by us, but by everybody else concerned. At times, it seems incredible when I recall the amount of thought and discussion that had to go into absolutely everything, but then all of those things were being done for the first time and caution had to be the watchword. It would have been unheard of to act on impulse on anything, no matter how trivial. On the subject of the medical bureau, Dr Gilmartin, who was open to reasonable suggestions at all times, thought the whole idea of medical investigation a very prudent one, and he asked us to take steps to make a beginning with its foundation.

Dr Stafford Johnson was at that time president of the Dublin branch of the Guild of SS Luke, Cosmos and Damien, a body of Catholic doctors who monitored any moral questions that were likely to arise across the whole field of medical matters. On his return to Dublin, he read a paper about Knock for its members; by then he had made himself familiar with all the information he required on the subject. During his stay with us he had more or less played the role of devil's advocate to make his mind clear about everything and when he left us, he had little doubt about all he had come to find out. To the end of his days however, he frequently played that part, whether to tease me or to fortify his own conviction I shall never know. He was a staunch friend to us and to Knock and remained so until his death a few years ago.

Very quickly, the formalities were agreed upon, the doctors moved with commendable speed and soon the medical bureau was established, with panels of doctors in Dublin and Galway. The duty roster, which included some of the most distinguished medical men and women in their special fields was then drawn up, and they, with Dr Stafford Johnson as president, and Dr George Maguire of Claremorris as secretary, attended for duty at Knock on their appointed days. In those days, all the doctors who served on the bureau attended at Knock on their agreed Sunday, exactly as the handmaids and stewards do today. A few of the Dublin doctors took their commitment very seriously, and came almost every Sunday, travelling down on the trains with the pilgrims. One of them, Dr Gallen, together with his brother, also a doctor, even took the trouble to design the invalid coaches and made himself available to consult with CIE during the time the prototype was being made. Meetings of the bureau were held in a room in St Mary's Hostel, and there the rules and working methods were set out. It is worthwhile noting that all of that medical expertise and everything else connected with the bureau was organised for the shrine on a voluntary basis.

It was firmly laid down then that pilgrimage organisers must provide medical certificates for any sick pilgrims who were coming to Knock on their particular pilgrimage to pray for a cure. This information, which gave the pilgrim's age and medical history, was provided by each one's own doctor, and was then filed at the medical bureau. Should any claim for improvement or healing have arisen subsequently, the facts were there for examination and comparison, a course of action which was designed to put an end to doubt and at the same time, any possible sensational rumour. Extreme care was exercised by all medical personnel regarding any claims, and no statement was issued for a very long time, quite a few years, afterwards.

It is understandably difficult for doctors to state that any patient is incurable, even more difficult to verify a claim to a miraculous cure. It goes against all their principles and their training. Yet, it must be said that those particular medical men, each with a well-earned reputation to uphold, examined and reported on several cases at Knock, with findings often at variance with expected prognosis. The medical bureau served us well in those early days, as it put an end to irresponsible claims and reporting. Much the same practice applies today, extreme caution is observed when examining and reporting on any claim to a miraculous cure, and a considerable length of time must elapse before a final medical opinion is given. Another facet of the work of those doctors was providing first-aid lectures for handmaids and stewards at Knock and at other local centres all through the winter months. It says much for their calibre and generosity that they were willing to give such an amount of their time to this worthy work, which I again stress, was voluntary.

During those years, we had a very varied and very interesting collection of people coming to stay with us in Bridgemount. We had artists, doctors, writers, priests, in fact we had people of many callings, but in one way or another, they all had something to contribute to the development of Knock. The discussions usually began at breakfast, then, when the time came to go to court, Liam left us, and joined us again when he had cleared up the work that awaited him on his return. Sometimes we would take them for a drive to some local beauty spot, but organising hospitality was for me, almost a whole time job. We would sit after a meal in the evening at the long dining-room table, the room fragrant with the perfume of freshly gathered roses or sweet pea, while the candles flickered as we talked and the evening darkened into a soft summer night. Plans for the gable shrine, publications, book-jackets or uniforms were made and talked about and, if the company happened to include priests and theologians, practicalities were put aside and the symbolism of the Apparition, or maybe facts about other Marian shrines came up for discussion. In those early days, that symbolism had not yet been fully interpreted so it generated its share of analytical argument. Ideas for expansion were put forward and subsequently, many of them were acted upon. Eventually, all talking done, we would trail up the stairs to bed. Where we put all such contrasting people to sleep, I just don't remember, but we did, and everything seemed to work out very well.

Among the many who came to stay with us around that time was Kathleen Flynn from Co. Roscommon. Her's was one of the first major cures which became known in our early days, and her case and medical history had been well recorded. I had heard about her cure very early on from several people and as the Second Commission of Enquiry was about to be set up, I wrote to her brother, Dominick, enquiring if there was any possibility of contacting her as it was proposed that her statement also should be taken and examined again. He was only too pleased to help, and before long, it was arranged that Kathleen would return from London where she was then nursing, to talk to us, and, what was more important, she was quite prepared to give evidence before the commission.

The plan was that she would stay with us, and as soon as the travel arrangements had been more or less completed and the day for her arrival drew near, I wrote and told her that I would meet her bus at Ballyhaunis and bring her here. Since we didn't know each other, I gave her the registration number of my car and described what I planned to wear, taking care to decide on something that would be easily recognisable. When the day came, I drove to Ballyhaunis and waited for the bus. Then, when it came and the passengers began to alight – there were not very many of them – I saw Kathleen, whom I recognised at once from her photograph. I went towards her and greeted her, but a very obvious hesitation in her manner told me that something was wrong. We got into the car and almost as soon as I began to move Kathleen said that she was so disappointed that Mrs Coyne had not come to meet her as promised and had sent somebody else. I assured her that I was Mrs Coyne, but she replied that she had been 'too long around to believe that', and in truth, nothing I could say could convince her otherwise.

The conversation on the way home, the best part of an hour's drive in those days, was almost monosyllabic on her part, and I wondered what sort of odd person she was, and how on earth I was going to cope with her for several days,

maybe even for a couple of weeks. We had Dr Stafford Johnson and Fr Angelus, the famous Capuchin, staying with us
at the time, and I didn't relish the prospect of having a
problem guest. Arrived at Bridgemount, Kathleen was shown
to her room and the usual courtesies extended to her. In
due course, we all assembled for our evening meal and Kathleen was introduced to the others. Not quite knowing what
might happen next, I steered them towards the dining-room,
but as nobody suspected that anything was amiss, everybody chatted normally, except for Kathleen who remained
very quiet.

I sat at the head of the table to keep an eye on the
guests, inwardly baffled as to how we were going to deal
with this new silent addition to our company when, about
halfway through the first course, Kathleen burst out suddenly, 'Now I believe you, you are Mrs Coyne'. The others,
unaware of the problems of the journey, were surprised, but
they did not have to wait very long for an explanation.
Kathleen went on to tell us in all seriousness that she had
been quite certain that I had sent somebody else to meet
her. 'Mrs Coyne' she told us, was fixed firmly in her mind
as 'a severe elderly lady, who would be wearing a tweed suit
with a long jacket, boots with buttons on one side, straight
grey hair pulled into a bun, with a sailor hat perched on
top', and, as a fashionable etcetera, 'she would be carrying
a rolled umbrella'. At this, all the others just exploded in
laughter and could hardly believe what they were hearing.
It didn't present a very inviting picture as she painted it,
and I truly wondered how she had agreed to come to spend
some time with such an unattractive creature. I suppose the
nature of my letters, coupled with the purpose of her visit
could reasonably have conjured up such an image, but in
the weeks that followed we laughed plenty about her imagined hostess. Still very young, and that evening probably

wearing a light summer dress, I could appreciate that she might have had a problem. She was not monosyllabic after that, as she turned out to have a tremendous personality, full of fun at all times. She and Dr Stafford Johnson hit it off very well, he teased her constantly about her cure, laughing at it from time to time, trying to find a weakness in her story, but on that story Kathleen was adamant and crystal clear.

Very early in her visit, she told all of us one evening the amazing story of her cure. As a very young girl, she had developed back trouble, and before long she had to consult local doctors who gave her little help. In 1921, she went to New York to stay with an aunt, in the hope that she might find some light work, but above all, some doctor who could give her relief from her pain. There, her condition deteriorated rapidly, and before long, she was admitted to the Metropolitan Hospital, New York City, where her ailment was diagnosed as Potts Disease. In those days, long before the discovery of effective treatment, there was very little that could be done for tuberculosis. She was given a plaster jacket to support her back, but after three months in hospital, she was discharged, and sent back to Ireland classified as a 'sick alien'. Compassion was a rare commodity in those days, no doubt it still might be in such circumstances!

Back home, her condition worsened rapidly and she was soon admitted to St Vincent's Hospital in Dublin, where the American diagnosis was confirmed. There she was given a new plaster jacket, but it proved to be no help either. She then went to yet another specialist, who this time took her into Baggot Street Hospital, where a stronger type of support was prescribed, but to no avail. She was then taken home to Castlerea where very soon, and in great pain, she was confined to bed, lying on hard boards most of the time. It was a hopeless situation.

Kathleen's mother was getting old, they were small farmers, which meant that there were few comforts, and so she suffered greatly. As 15 August 1925 drew near, Kathleen asked her brother, Dominick, if he would take her to Knock on that day. It was a big thing to ask, as he had no means of transport and a hired car would cost a great deal. However, after much heart-searching he agreed. When the day came, Kathleen was too ill to travel, but on the sixteenth, she was feeling slightly stronger, so they set out. Having arrived at Knock, she lay in great pain and unable to move, then, halfway through Mass, she became very ill. At that point Dominick realised that there was little he could do but return home with, as he thought, his dying sister. All that night she was near to death, until at last, in the early hours of the morning, she fell asleep. Her mother, who had sat with her through the long night, had expected her death at every moment. Early next morning, Dominick, fearing that a funeral was imminent, and knowing very well that there was little in the house to pay for it or for any other necessities, set out with his bonhams to Castlerea market to sell them.

At midday Kathleen awoke, she was extremely uncomfortable and her jacket was causing her great pain. Unable to bear it any longer she felt an urge to get up, and as soon as she made a move to do so, she was forced by the pain to stand erect. At that moment, she discovered that she could use her limbs and that the agonising pain had left her. She ran to the kitchen where her exhausted mother had begun to doze by the fire. Waking at once when Kathleen entered, and now terrified that she was about to witness her death, she hardly heard as Kathleen told her that she was cured. She watched as she ran out of the house and into the adjoining field, where to her utter dismay, she saw her swing the stick she had been holding several times in an arc around her head and fling it as far as possible into the distance. She then came back into the house and proceeded to dress, this time without any assistance, announcing to her mother that she was going there and then to tell the priest, who also had been expecting news of her death, and without further delay, she walked off quickly down the road.

Somewhere along the way, Dominick, returning from the market, saw the sprightly young girl walking quickly towards him. Not recognising her he thought how like his sister she looked, in the years when that sister was well. She greeted him cheerfully and with great difficulty she managed to convince him that she was, in fact, Kathleen, and that she had been cured. She told us about all the excitement that followed and the joy of everybody around her that she was well again. The following Sunday she returned to Knock to give thanks and to place her plaster jacket inside the railings of the church at the gable, a common practice in those days.

All of those facts had been documented, with medical certificates from New York and Vincent's Hospitals to prove her condition in 1922 and 1923. Since her cure, she had gone to London and trained as a nurse, there was no arrangement in those days for reporting her cure officially, or of recording her statement. A picture in *Knock Shrine* shows her during her training, robust and smiling in her nurse's uniform. Now in 1936, fully trained and working normally, she came forward to report enthusiastically and with deep gratitude on her wonderful cure. She came to us that summer a picture of health and full of life. She stayed with us for quite a little while and her light-heartedness was a tonic to all of us. Some time after her return to London, she opened her own nursing home, where she continued to attend to the sick through the war years, even as the bombs fell. There were no half measures about that particular cure.

From that summer on when the medical bureau was first founded, we have always taken great care to ensure that a doctor is on call on every big pilgrimage day. Today there is a resident doctor at Knock and several within close range, and there is always an ambulance on stand-by, very different from the early days. From the beginning also we have had a big number of trained nurses among the general body of handmaids and it has always been the practice to have several on duty during pilgrimages. We have many nurses among our ranks, some with very impressive special-ised training, which is always useful. Apart from the days of large crowds, there can always be the unexpected accident or illness, and one must be ready to deal with it. In the early days, the situation was comparable in relation to pilgrim numbers.

Today, the medical bureau is examining the case of Marian Carroll, a young woman who, in 1972 became seri-ously ill with an illness diagnosed in due course as Multiple Sclerosis. For almost seventeen years she endured great pain and a general impairment of her faculties until, 3 September 1989, when unable to walk, to swallow her food or control her bodily functions, she was taken to Knock. During Mass and the Blessing of the Sick she felt very ill and abandoned, realising that she would soon be taken from her husband and children. She prayed fervently to Our Lady, begging her, as a mother, to help her. After Holy Communion she got an intense pain in her feet, then, almost as quickly, every pain she had, left her. In her own words she tells us she felt 'this beautiful feeling like a whispering breeze tell-ing me that if the stretcher was opened for me I could get up and walk'. As soon as Mass was over she was taken to St John's Rest and Care Centre where she asked a nurse if she could open her stretcher for her, which she did. At once, Marian stood up and walked. The muscles that had been wasted in her legs had become perfect, her whole body was healed. One of the handmaids handed her a cup of tea, which she took and casually drank, then realised that until that moment she had been unable to drink. At that point, one of the handmaids came and asked me to come with her as there was something I should see. I spoke to Marian, and not realising what was happening, I handed her an *Annual*, remarking that she might like to read it. The *Annual* fell open at an article entitled 'Why is the rosary so powerful?' Marian took it and read out the title, saying 'Isn't that strange, we always had great devotion to the rosary in our family', but stranger still was the fact that Marian, who had gradually lost her sight, had, until that moment, been unable to read.

In cases like this, we, the handmaids, and indeed all staff dealing with the sick, even though we may be amazed and delighted, are instructed to keep a calm exterior and avoid any fuss, and so it was. Marian went home from Knock that evening to tell her husband and her children of her amazing cure. Today, she is a handmaid herself, in full health working among the sick, dispensing care, hope and courage while she prays with them. She also travels all round the world speaking to thousands on the power of prayer and healing, while the doctors examine and evaluate her case in accordance with very strict guidelines. For Marian, however, the case is crystal clear, she was at death's door and now she is well, happy, and full of praise for the wonders of the Lord.

To return to those early years: in 1936, it was decided to hold the Second Commission of Enquiry, to ensure yet again, while some of the witnesses were still alive, that all evidence would be absolutely clear and that no detail, however trivial it might appear to be, would be missed. Before it was convened, there was a great deal of discussion about it between Liam, the canon and the archbishop. Between them they decided that this time statements should be taken on oath, and so it was, a commissioner for oaths was present to put a legal seal on all the proceedings.

By that time, Mrs O'Connell, the principal witness was getting on in years, and her health was failing, so the matter had become urgent. When eventually the commissioners got together to take the statements it was necessary for them to come to Knock to do so. There was no question of Mrs O'Connell being strong enough to go to Tuam as she was then confined to bed. We went over to Knock on the day she was to be examined and I remember going upstairs to the chapel in St Mary's Hostel, the room in which Archdeacon Cavanagh had died, and we prayed that all would go well for her. On that occasion, she finished her evidence with the spontaneous words before she signed the document, 'I make this statement on my death-bed, knowing that I am soon to go before my God'. As it so happened, she did not live for very long after that.

The two other witnesses who were then still alive, Patrick Byrne and John Curry were also examined before the commission. Patrick Byrne was examined at Knock, but John Curry, who had been only six years old or so at the time of the Apparition, had emigrated to New York and was still living there. He was then elderly, and there was no question of his returning home, so by arrangement with the commission he gave his evidence, also under oath, in New York.

All of that took a considerable length of time, but once again, the witnesses were considered 'upright and trustworthy'. The findings were sent to Rome by Dr Gilmartin three years later, in 1939.

6

Flowers for Knock
Gold for the crown
Taking statements and signatures
Frank Duff

M eantime, behind the scenes, the work went on. At the first meeting of our new committee, the Society for Promoting the Cause of Knock, I had been voted to be organising secretary, and soon words had to become deeds and plans had to materialise. We bought another typewriter and I sat down and worked at learning how to use it properly. I had been taught typing while at school, but nobody could say that I was efficient. However, I soon got the hang of it – I had little choice. Liam already typed pretty well as he wrote quite a lot and typed everything first time around. Very quickly my learning days had to end and it became necessary to type letters and replies to letters, which grew from a trickle at the beginning to a torrent as the campaign progressed. We had a large settee in the hall and every morning it was filled by the postman with the morning's incoming mail, but by some miracle, and with a great deal of work, we managed to cope with it and clear it.

Some little time ago, I ordered a quantity of heavy decorating material in town and as they were awkward to carry to the car, the shop owner very kindly offered to deliver them. Later that evening he drove up with the purchases and when he carried them into the hall, he asked whoever answered the door if Mrs Coyne still lived here. On being told that she did, he appeared to be very interested and told her that he had once worked in the post office in town and he remembered sorting out usually a hundred, frequently even up to two hundred letters for the Coynes at this address each morning. Over the years I suppose I must have written hundreds of thousands of words in various forms, from simple replies to letters to complicated drafts for this and that. It adds up to a gigantic volume of writing however one might look at it. As I recall, we replied to letters quickly enough but even so, there was then still time for other things, though I must admit that even those soon became Knock related.

In the long summer evenings, if nobody happened to be staying with us, we continued to make plans and now and then, I would put everything else aside and make an effort to do some of the routine jobs in the house or garden such as jam-making in season and the occasional bout of special cooking. We had not been all that long in the house at the time, it was still at the stage of being put together and naturally, I loved to give it as much attention as I could. One fine sunny day in the spring, Pat came into the house to show me the beautiful aster plants he had raised under glass in the warmth of the orchard, where, shaded by high stone walls, one could always find a sunny spot. He was very proud of them and was about to plant them when I realised that he seemed to have a huge number of boxes and containers stacked ready for action. I asked him how many plants he had and he told me that he had around two thousand, enough to fill the whole length of the beds in the front of the house. The thought of this beautiful carpet of colour in the autumn was too much for me and, putting the work I had in hand aside, I went and changed shoes and whatever else was necessary and arrived on the lawn in full gardening gear to plant the asters with Pat. We worked steadily all day, stopping for only the briefest spells to eat, much to the amusement of Liam who got great fun out of my occasional bursts of enthusiastic gardening, though I found it very rewarding, as I loved seeing things growing and taking shape. That evening, very sore, but very satisfied, I came inside, delighted with my day's work.

Early next morning, even before I went to Mass, I ran out to have a quick look at the asters to see how they had fared in the darkness. I simply couldn't believe my eyes, and I ran quickly all the way down the path to make sure that I was seeing correctly. Not one leaf remained of our two thousand beautiful plants. The rabbits had come in the night, or at daybreak, or whenever it is that rabbits come, and had eaten every single one, down to the last stalk. Pat, who was usually reasonably philosophical about the occasional raids from marauding pests and livestock, was for once left speechless, indeed on that particular day, he had the greatest difficulty in containing his temper, and he muttered eloquently to himself words I was not supposed to hear, but who could have blamed him!

Apart from the asters, which were mainly ornamental, we always grew quantities of flowers for Knock. Before long, it was not possible to accommodate all we needed in the formal garden in front of the house, so the kitchen garden at the back, which had been our main space for vegetables, was put into service. There, beside the raspberry canes, Pat dug drills and planted gladioli, dahlias, delphiniums and everything else which we considered suitable for cutting. The drills are still there, overgrown now with moss and grass, but I do not now have the flowers. Gardening on that scale needs the full time attention of at least one man, more realistically, two.

We also grew sweet pea in abundance along the tall wire fence of the tennis court and across a rose pergola which we had in those days. One particular year, possibly because the weather was just right, or maybe because the ground was fresh and newly prepared, the blooms were especially splendid, large, lush and in every shade imaginable. One memorable morning when they were at their very best, in fact they were a real picture, Liam and I drove in from Mass in Ballinafad, and as soon as we rounded a bend on the avenue we sensed, in the peculiar way one senses these things, that something was amiss. We didn't have to wait very long to discover what it was. Standing on their hind legs, their mouths full of the last of the sweet pea, were Dolly and her kid, Nanny, two frolicsome goats that had strayed into us some time before and had very quickly become pets. The kid was a delightful, playful little creature that frequently scampered up the front steps on her dainty feet and loved to be hand fed. On that particular morning, they had escaped from their quarters and, as they came bounding to meet us, it was obvious that they had had a splendid time, but I wasn't so sure about their charm just at that particular moment. Pat was of course eloquent, though resigned, as from the beginning he had his doubts about the goats, and his 'What did I tell you!' was no surprise. Those natural disasters however, were not the things that bothered us then. They happened to us, and though they were a nuisance at the time, they were quickly forgotten, and one began again.

The demand for flowers for the shrine and the processional statue grew, with more and still more pilgrimage days, which soon extended through the whole summer right into autumn, until it became quite impossible to grow sufficient amounts. I was beginning to wonder where I could turn to for flowers, when I remembered Sr Margaret Mary Brett, a St Louis sister, who was then at their convent in Kiltimagh. I had known Sr Margaret Mary for years, indeed her family had been near neighbours and she had been a friend for as long as I could remember. As a child, I was sent to St Louis Convent in Balla for a short time before I went as a boarder to the Dominicans in Taylor's Hill, Galway. While in Balla, Sr Margaret Mary was always there to confide in and to give consolation on the occasions when I had been at the receiving end of what then appeared to have been rough justice. In the 1930s, she was an old, or what appeared to me then to be, an old nun. She was tall and dignified with a great air of authority. On the day I first called on her and asked her about flowers, she led me without a moment's hesitation to the garden, almost as if I was still her pupil. Together we moved up and down the paths among the beds of beautiful flowers, chatting about friends and neighbours, while she cut armloads of blooms, putting them in little piles to be collected at the end of our harvesting and given to me. Saturday after Saturday, I went to her, it seems to me now, almost shamelessly, but she always gave generously.

Around that time, the Sisters of St John of God bought Ballinamore House, which stands a few miles from Kiltimagh, and is, as far as I know, now used by the Western Health Board. In the beginning, the sisters had it as a novitiate for their order, and later they ran a nursing home there. We already knew the house, in fact we had vaguely considered buying it when we were first house hunting, but decided it was too big. One day it came into my mind for some reason and, remembering its beautiful gardens, I decided to call on the sisters and ask them if they would give us flowers. I need not have stopped to question it, as they did so without hesitation. Saturdays on my way to Knock I called at Ballinamore, when Sr Josephine and I would go together into the high-walled gardens and cut the most exquisite blossoms, carrying them to the car in quantities, until the back, and frequently the boot as well, were full. It was an incredible car load, which in today's terms would be worth hundreds of pounds, but the sisters thought nothing of it, the flowers were for Our Lady, and that was the end of it.

My almost life-long habit of driving station-wagon type cars began because of the need to carry these huge quantities of flowers, my normal Saturday load.

In those days also, Mrs Mullaghy, who lived in Castlebar, would go around to every house which she knew to have a garden to ask for flowers, and she was rarely refused. Each Saturday night the hall in Bridgemount was packed tight with flowers, varying as the summer came to fullness and faded. The perfume of the pale waxy orange blossoms which grow along the avenue and which we still cut during the early months of the summer, fills the house even yet in the warm evenings. It is for me now almost a symbol of Knock and its processional statue. We have been cutting it for as long as I can remember. Down through the years, people from all over the country have given flowers most generously to Knock. I remember all of them, too numerous to mention, who came several times each season, with a profusion of choice blooms for the shrine. Some grew them especially for this purpose, others spent large sums in purchasing them. Decorating the statue, which in 1954 was solemnly crowned with full papal authority, was a practice we began in the 1930s, at the time it first arrived.

Some years ago, new arrangements were made about the flowers and the statue, as a professional landscape gardener, Anne Lavin, had been appointed at Knock, and now takes care of all the floral requirements and does them beautifully. Long years ago, I remember making a suggestion about the provision of a garden, or in some way trying to beautify the church precinct, but like many of our suggestions at the time, it was the cause of great amusement. Still, I suppose the time had not come for such plans, at that stage we had no proper shrine, nor even the ground to develop or consider the like, but it is good to have lived to see these things now taking shape. Anne, together with her staff, plan and lay out the magnificent pattern of flowers which have become such a joy to everybody, and in the summer she frequently has sufficient freshly grown flowers for all church purposes. Considering our unpredictable climate, this is quite an achievement, since delicate blooms sometimes have to take a cruel battering from the wind and rain. It all adds up to an immense amount of flower cultivation, but the results are greatly appreciated by the pilgrims, who seem to make the statue the number one picture when they come to focus their cameras.

The African Mission College at Ballinafad was a flourishing secondary school for the SMA students when we moved to Bridgemount, and it had a number of resident priests to look after the boys and their classes. From the moment we bought the house, in fact even before we finalised the deal, we had obtained permission from our parish priest in Balla and from the SMA fathers themselves to attend daily Mass there. The fact that we could do so was the deciding factor in the purchase of Bridgemount. We could perhaps have gone to Mass in the village, but it would have been a real problem as Mass was fixed for an hour much too late to begin work afterwards. Ballinfad was therefore a God-send to us, to be able to slip up there, less than a mile away, and to hear Mass quietly at seven or seven-thirty in the morning, with plenty of time left for everything. The priests often came down to join us for a meal of an evening and to meet our guests or, their day's work done, they sometimes called casually for a chat or a cup of coffee at night.

One evening, Fr Harry Sheppard, at the time he was superior in the college, called to see us, and told us that he and the staff were proposing a walking pilgrimage to Knock for the boys. Such an outing meant a walk each way of around eighteen miles at least, and as the boys' ages covered the normal secondary school span, which included some who were still quite young, it seemed to be a very big undertaking. However, towards the end of the summer term that year, the intrepid company, at least the hardier among them, set out to tramp the long road to Knock. From a couple of pictures of them in an early *Annual* they seem to have gone about it in style, not as youngsters would today, wearing comfortable jeans, tee shirts and anoraks, but in full fig, with jackets, collars and ties, and, to make it really difficult, they carried a banner. No doubt in those days of rigid discipline and mandatory uniforms, they probably had little choice. One of them wrote a piece for the *Annual* for us afterwards describing the outing and filled in details as the boys would have seen them, and it appeared to have been a worthwhile exercise which they enjoyed. Fr Sheppard and Fr Beirne escorted them, also on foot, going along the bog road through Loona and on to Balla, reciting the rosary, with suitable meditations, as they progressed. By arrangement, the St John of God Sisters gave them lunch in Ballinamore, then they continued to Kiltimagh and on to Knock. That night, when prayers were finished, they wrapped themselves in blankets and slept on the floor of the old school, with those who could not be accommodated there packing themselves into the invalids' hut. Next day after Mass and breakfast, they walked back to Ballinafad, praying on the homeward journey as they had done on their way to Knock, and I read that on their return, the cook rewarded them magnificently. It was a splendid effort and they achieved their goal, though I am quite sure that they did not themselves consider it a great hardship.

Sometime around then, we had our first Irish-speaking pilgrimage. It was a new and very unusual undertaking and it was initiated by people whose names were very well known then in the Irish-speaking world. The pilgrimage continues to this day, organised by 'An Realt', the Irish-speaking section of the Legion of Mary. That first occasion, however, was memorable. Pilgrims came from Dublin and from all over the country, but particularly they came from the Gaeltacht and from the islands. The distinctive shawls of the women from Aran added a unique sense of colour and occasion that day, as some old photographs in the *Annual* plainly show. The Aran shawl is now no more than a museum piece, but in its time it must have been a most beautiful and comfortable garment. The music, however, was the glory of that day, indeed for many days: Máire Ní Scolai, the famous traditional singer of her time, possibly the first in that line, and Fr Joseph Higgins, later Monsignor Higgins of the diocese of Achonry, backed by a choir from St Louis Convent, Kiltimagh, gave a magnificent rendering of 'Caoine na dTrí Mhuire', the Lament of the Three Marys. It was sung during the Stations of the Cross, replacing the then usual 'Stabat Mater'. Máire's clear and hauntingly beautiful soprano voice blended perfectly with Fr Higgins's rich tones, two superb artists, their glorious notes floating out over the crowds on our newly acquired amplification system. It was a moment of rare beauty and serene dignity, a memory that I shall always cherish.

Following some of the endless discussions that took place during those eventful summers, an idea was put forward that we should collect gold and precious stones from the people of Ireland, and when we had sufficient, we should have a crown made from them for the processional statue, which had just been made by Earleys, the then renowned church artists of Dublin. An early *Knock Shrine Annual* carries the announcement of the plan and the following year, a list of people who had by then begun to donate gifts is given. It is an interesting and touching comment on the times – one finds a name, followed by 'engagement ring, diamond and sapphire', 'ear-rings, gold chain and bangle, 'brooch of emeralds', 'mother's wedding ring', 'father's tie pin', all valuable and valued possessions; cherished mementos of dear ones, yet given to us with faith and singular generosity to make a fitting crown for Our Lady of Knock.

Also included in that list is an acknowledgement to Mrs K. Kirwan from Dublin for 'a large amethyst cut and set in gold and rescued from a desecrated shrine in Russia'. In a separate article, Mrs Kirwan told, at our request, the story of having been offered the amethyst by a Russian émigré five years before. He had made no secret of the fact that the stone had been looted from the shrine of the Vladimir Madonna in Moscow, and he was offering it for sale. Having established that the circumstances surrounding it were genuine, she purchased it, naively thinking that she might somehow be allowed to go to Moscow and restore it to its original setting. Going to Moscow was not a particular problem at that time, but restoring a jewel to a desecrated shrine was another story. Full of the idea, however, she set out in due course and having got there, she learned that the two most venerated pictures of Our Lady in Russia were in Moscow. One of these, Our Lady of Vladimir, was in the Church of the Assumption which was within the Kremlin, a fact which indicated the importance of the icon in the days before the plundering began. At the time of Mrs Kirwan's visit that church had been closed. She asked for permission to visit it, and strange to tell, it was quickly granted, but just as quickly, it was withdrawn. Instead, she was taken to an art museum which contained icons which had been cleaned and restored, but stripped of their jewelled shrines, and there among them, she found the ancient picture of Our Lady of Vladimir. The guide described it to her as the oldest and most historic Madonna in Russia, and in the course of her visit to the museum Mrs Kirwan purchased a picture of the icon, but predictably, all efforts to visit the church failed.

Bitterly disappointed, she returned to Ireland bringing the amethyst with her, but determined to go back to Russia to restore the jewel at a future date, next time with all the required permissions. Meantime, war had been declared, and all hope of completing such a mission was dashed. Some little time after her return, she was talking one evening with Countess O'Byrne and she told her the story of her disappointing experience. The countess listened to her with great interest, and then she told her about the proposed Knock crown suggesting that she might consider donating her amethyst to it. Mrs Kirwan was very taken by the account of Knock, about which she knew little or nothing, and before very long she decided that as it would probably be years before she could get back to Russia, she felt that Our Lady would not mind if she presented the jewel to her crown at Knock. She gave it to us then, believing that in return, to quote her own words, 'with the help and prayer of our people, Our Lady of Knock will replace the jewel of faith in the persecuted soul of the Russian people'. As things are now turning out, it may not be all that long before that prayer is answered.

It took fourteen years for the crown to become a reality, not because the gifts were in any way slow in coming to us, far from it, people were most generous and we soon had plenty for our purpose. However, we were still in the era when it was difficult to get things done, and it never seemed to be the right time as far as some things we proposed were concerned.

As Europe stood in that uneasy period before war was declared, the taking of statements and the full findings of the Second Commission of Enquiry were being completed, but before it was ready to be sent to Rome, we were faced with a new and immense amount of work. It was decided that accounts of cures should accompany the submission, so full reports and documentation had to be provided. That was not too bad, as it had been done not all that long before for inclusion in the book, and by that time there was a medical bureau to substantiate claims, but that was by no means our only commitment. When sending the submission was first agreed on in 1936, it was decided to request people from all over Ireland to sign a petition for its success. I don't remember if it was a novel idea then, but it has become a common enough practice today. We wrote a standard letter and sent sheets for signatures to reliable and trusted canvassers in all areas and we ended up with an enormous response. The areas targeted were naturally the most influential, beginning with both houses of the Oireachtas, members of Northern Ireland parliament, the judiciary, the universities, the army, local government, counts of the Holy See who were then quite numerous, distinguished Knights of Malta, distinguished Irish people living in England, architects, medical and other professional people, as well as the ordinary citizens of the country, lay people all. We ended up with a very comprehensive list of worthy laity.

While it was being collected, a St Louis sister, Sr Bernadette in Kiltimagh convent, at our request, planned and painted a design in gold onto the cover of white satin, while Sr Angela of the same convent did the script of the petition in Irish and English. It all added up to a very large book which we then had bound by O'Gormans in Galway, and we had a facsimile copy bound in leather which I still have.

After a great deal of work and the undreamed of final time-consuming details, it was finished and almost as we finished it, it suddenly became urgent. One morning at the height of the finalising the archbishop sent us a telegram asking us to get it to him in Tuam as quickly as possible and, almost by a miracle, we were able to arrange to finish it and to go there next morning.

As it happened, trying to send the findings of that commission to Rome could not have come at a worse moment. Communication with any part of Europe was then almost impossible, as people, realising the inevitable, stayed at home while the world watched and waited. By some extraordinary accident, Frank Duff, the founder of the Legion of Mary, was at that moment making final plans for a journey to Rome on important Legion business. The Church authorities who then knew all about his plans saw in him an ideal courier who could take the documents safely. This, he all too readily and perhaps foolishly agreed to do. We were told about this and, like all concerned, were almost afraid to consider the outcome. However, on the inside cover of the copy of the petition which I have, there is a handwritten card posted in Tuam a few days afterwards, with the words, 'Parcel arrived safely in Rome, I have just got acknowledgement', and signed + JW, who was of course Dr Walsh, then the archbishop elect. I clearly remember the day we received that card, and the relief it was to know that that particular part of the work had been completed.

However, it had not all been plain sailing for Frank Duff. He had not for one moment, considered the full implications and delicate nature of that particular assignment. He was given a large black box, securely sealed, which he was instructed to deliver safely to a specified office within the Vatican. As travel was entirely by land in those days, every frontier presented a challenge. He was carrying a box of secret documents and had only the vaguest knowledge about its contents. It was not the best passport for such an inadequately briefed traveller, and inevitably he was treated with the utmost suspicion at every point. The extraordinary thing about all of it was that despite the danger, the relentless watchfulness on the part of the authorities, and though everything else he carried was examined thoroughly, at no point along the way was that box opened. Afterwards, he realised fully the danger he might have been in on such an unsolicited mission, and when eventually he felt free to talk, he told us about it with all its 'might have beens' embellished by his own special brand of humour. Before that he said, he had not been a great believer in Knock, but after it, he was quite convinced that it had at least one miracle.

Looking back on all of this, and it is perhaps only at this distance that one is able to recall with meaningful perspective the number of contrasting people from so many different backgrounds who, one way or another were called, and who found themselves to be in the position of being able to answer that call, to further the promotion of Knock shrine at the precise moment when each one's particular type of help and talent was absolutely vital.

7

Diamond Jubilee 1939
Archbishop Gilmartin
Wartime conditions

I n 1939, while still a very new society, we celebrated the
diamond jubilee of the Apparition. Plans were laid months
in advance and in due course details were made known to
the daily papers, which in those days, were generous in their
coverage of Knock, so a lot of people were able to read about
it.

For the Vigil of the Feast of 21 August, the anniversary
of the Apparition, there was a candlelight procession, a big
event then, and that particular occasion had its own very
special charm. As there was no outside public lighting, the
light was the light from the moon, which that night was
magical, and the flickering river of flame from the hundreds
of candles, as it meandered slowly around the old church.
Above all else, the silence and peace of that still night provided the ideal setting for the long hours of meditation and
prayer. It gave us plenty of time to think about the plans we
had in hand, and all we might be called on to do in the future, which in those early days presented a somewhat daunt-
ing prospect.

The gable wall of the old church was then bare and unattractive, so very early in the planning, it was decided to
decorate it with scrolls which were to be made from thick
ropes of fresh green moss. Though this might sound very
'folksy' and makeshift, it was anything but, and in the end
the whole thing was quite beautiful and very effective. We
had given the project an immense amount of thought in

advance and, when we finally got around to doing it, some amongst us spent days gathering moss from the barks of old trees, and from every nook and cranny in the woods, then securing it around strands of twisted hay which were used to form the letters. Silk flowers were fastened into the moss and finally the ropes were gently eased into position and secured on to huge lengths of wire mesh, long enough to stretch the full width of the gable, spelling out the words which Bridget Trench had called to the Virgin Mary on that night sixty years before, 'Céad fáilte a Mhuire'.

When we first took the measurements we knew that it would be impossible to accommodate those long lengths of wire in a normal house, and we had a problem trying to decide where all this could be carried out. In the end it was all laid out on the wooden floor of the granary. It was high summer and the weather was warm, so working there and being able to see the pattern as it took shape was rather pleasant for all concerned. It was also very satisfactory to be able to leave everything in position while we did something else, and then find it undisturbed when we returned. When the scrolls were finished, and eventually fastened securely to the wall, they looked wonderful, their splendid colours bringing the old grey gable to life. They hung there for weeks, even when the flowers had long faded, as Canon Grealy liked them so much that he wouldn't let anybody take them down.

On the day of the Jubilee, 21 August, Mass was said at the temporary altar at the side of the church. Seats were taken out for the special guests to kneel on, come rain, come sun, and as it happened, it was sunny. The guests included Mr Tom Deirg, TD, Minister for Education, and Mrs Deirg; Mr W. Cosgrave, TD; Mr Frank Carty, TD; Mr J. Mongan, TD; as well as Count and Countess O'Byrne. Several distinguished members of the Knights of Malta were present, and to add to the excitement and prestige of the day, the whole ceremony was broadcast. The processional statue, which we used until some years ago, and which earlier that day had been blessed by Canon Grealy, was carried in procession for the first time. It was estimated that around 30,000 pilgrims attended, and for those times that was a huge number. It was the first big pilgrimage or special event we had organised, and though it had more than its share of disappointments and frustrations unpleasant in the extreme, it nonetheless proved that objectives could be achieved with hard work, patience, a great deal of diplomacy, but above all, prayer.

Later on that season, sometime in the early autumn, Liam and I went to Tuam one day to an 'Aeridheacht' – a sort of open air entertainment common enough at the time – which was being held in the grounds of the cathedral. I've forgotten why exactly it was held, probably for some worthy cause, but it was planned as a big event. It was a fine, warm sunny day and we were enjoying ourselves meeting and talking to friends when, early in the afternoon, Fr Fergus, who was secretary to the archbishop, came to us and told us that the archbishop had seen us in the crowd and he would very much like to talk to us if we could spare the time and would care to join him for a cup of tea. The archbishop had a great eye for seeing people and rarely missed anything. We said to Fr Fergus that we would be delighted to come, but when he had left us, and we got a chance of a quiet word together, we wondered what the archbishop might want to say to us. After a little time, at what seemed a reasonable moment to leave, we made our excuses to friends and headed for his house, or palace, as it was then called.

We found Dr Gilmartin in good spirits and he welcomed us warmly. We chatted in a general way for a little time and when tea was finished and we were talking freely, he said that he had been thinking very seriously for a long time about Knock, and wanted to talk to us alone about it, as he had some very important things to say. He seemed for that moment to have laid aside his official mantle, and proceeded to talk to us quite informally, indeed as it appeared to us, almost confidentially. He wanted us to know, he told us, that when Fr John Tuffy, who had been parish priest of Knock some years before, came to him one day way back in 1929, and asked him if he would be present at the Golden Jubilee ceremonies and meet the pilgrims who were coming from Dublin, he told Fr Tuffy that he could not be there, as the Church had not yet made any official pronouncement about the authenticity of the Apparition. At the time, he said, he was greatly concerned about it and was not at all sure about how it should be handled, though for twenty years, he had prayed about it constantly. At the end of all that deliberation he had, he said, made a pact with Our Lady that he would do nothing about Knock until the laity approached him and asked him to do so, as it seemed to be their particular responsibility.

He told us that he had felt very badly about having to refuse Fr Tuffy's request, but refuse he did. He then went on to tell us an extraordinary story. On the morning of the Golden Jubilee that August, when walking quietly up and down in the sunshine outside his house, saying his office, an internal voice seemed to positively command him to go to Knock, and that voice kept it up with a distinct rhythm, until he could ignore it no longer. Then without further hesitation he called his driver and asked him to get ready at once to go to Knock. Greatly surprised at the sudden decision, his driver asked him if he had informed Fr Tuffy, but the archbishop said that he had not, and as there was no method of so doing at that point, since there were no telephones, he said that it would just have to take its course.

He told us of how fervently he had prayed on the journey to Knock, asking for guidance along every mile of the way. As they approached the link road with Barnacarrol, which is a small and dangerous junction at the top of a hill on the Claremorris side of Knock, another car shot out at speed straight across their path. His driver braked rapidly, which put their car into a skid, while the other one went headlong off the road, and over the ditch on the far side. When they had all recovered from their initial shock, and taken stock of the situation, realising that nobody had been hurt, not even the erring driver, they were very grateful to God and continued on their journey. Then, after a long and thoughtful pause, he went on to tell us that in that split second of anticipating the seeming inevitable impact with the other car, he experienced an intense awareness of Our Lady's presence, almost as if she were stretching out to protect him. The incident, and the close encounter with death, shocked him greatly, and made him think very seriously about the merits or otherwise of his mission.

Later that night when he returned home, he spent an unusually long time in deliberation and prayer, after which, he told us, that he had renewed his pact with Our Lady about the shrine's promotion in the context of the laity. When, five years later, we came to him asking for permission to write a book, to found the Society for Promoting the Cause, and take on all the other activities such promotion might entail, he took it as a clear sign that his prayer had been answered.

At that stage in the interview we were both very surprised at the tone of the conversation, as in all the time we had been involved in working for Knock, we had not been favoured with many confidences. However, there was more to come. The archbishop then went on to tell us that as our bishop, there was very little he could have done to help us during the preceding years, but he wanted us to know that he was well aware of the difficulties we were encountering on every side. He hoped, he said, that we would be able to carry on with the work as we were doing it, and he assured us that we were very much in his prayers at all times. At the end of a very, very, long discussion, if indeed it could be so called, as he had done most of the talking, we imagined that everything had been said, and we stood up to leave. The archbishop, however, appeared to be still deep in thought and inclined to linger. Very slowly, he escorted us to the door, then, just as we were about to say goodbye he stopped, and after a little hesitation, he said that he could see Knock becoming a very important shrine in future years, and taking my hand, he said very earnestly that he believed that in my lifetime I would see a great church being built there, and it would one day become a centre of singular devotion. He then added that he was an old man and wouldn't live much longer, but that I would see all these great things come about. We were rather at a loss for something suitable to say, in such circumstances where might one find suitable words, so after the usual pleasantries, we knelt while he gave us his blessing and prayed for a continuing blessing on our work. Then without further discussion, we left.

The interview with Dr Gilmartin was entirely unexpected, and in many ways, not at all characteristic of the man. It impressed us deeply, but it also worried us quite a bit, and in the days that followed, we talked about it again and again. It was difficult to come to terms with such a conversation or to put it in perspective, especially in the light of everything that we had come to expect. If it had been intended as an effort to encourage us in the work, we wondered if he was being a bit over optimistic. If, on the other hand it was a firmly held opinion, we were at a loss to see how and when such developments might take place. All in all, it had been an extraordinary encounter, but one thing was heartening even if he had said nothing else, and that was the realisation that the archbishop had all along been so genuinely concerned about the entire question of Knock, which was a very welcome piece of information. Also, from what he had told us, he appeared to have been inspired in everything he had done, almost as if every move had been following some very special plan. Above everything else it was wonderful to realise that he stood firmly behind us, as there were many times in those days, when the discouragement from so many others sometimes tended to cloud our aims.

Dr Gilmartin had the reputation for being a cold, aloof man, but one of deep spirituality and holiness, and he was highly esteemed as a theologian. He had travelled abroad a great deal, something which was quite unusual for his time, and he was also very well read, and well known for his wide literary abilities. In the circumstances, his opinions on all serious matters were highly respected, particularly within his own circles. Over the weeks that followed, as we thought and spoke together about the conversation and tried to analyse it accurately, we could not help remembering the opinion of the two young priests who had been with us at Lourdes a few years before, who had given the opinion that we must not expect any action in the lifetime of this archbishop as he was 'too conservative'! Conservative, perhaps, but cautious might have been a better word. With hindsight it was almost inevitable that young clerics would have concluded that a man so remote from them in experience, years and rank, would have been conservative to say the least. During all that time however, unknown to anybody, either priests or people, he had pondered on and prayed quietly about the whole question of Knock, and was merely waiting for the right moment to do something about it.

He seemed to be in good health when we left him, we had not heard that he had been ill or in any way off form. He was working and carrying out his duties normally, and his general behaviour gave no cause at all for concern to anybody, or any reason to imagine that his days with us would be short. Certainly his wisdom and judgement seemed on that occasion to be solid and sharp in the extreme. However, bearing out his own words exactly, just a few weeks after that he died.

That year saw the outbreak of war in Europe and though we stood very much on its edge, there was no reason to believe that we would escape entirely. For the remainder of the year, and into 1940, plans were laid for a great national pilgrimage to pray for peace and the protection of Ireland. On 18 August 1940, thousands of people gathered to pray for those intentions. Mass cards representing ten thousand Masses offered throughout all the counties of Ireland, north and south, were placed at the shrine. Together with a couple of the handmaids, I placed them on the altar in flower-decked baskets early that morning, thirty-two of them, one for each county. It was a magnificent occasion, one of the highlights of those formative years.

The war dragged on and, thank God, barely touched us, yet, in our own way we had problems, but only in smaller things. There were shortages of all kinds, and rationing. Paper for the *Annual* and for other publications was almost impossible to get in sufficient quantity, but somehow we always managed to get some. Basic food was not scarce in rural areas, where one had one's own milk, butter, eggs, some meat, etc., though tea and coffee were on ration only, and beyond that, impossible to get, except of course on the black market, where one could get almost everything. There were certainly no luxuries, no fruit came from far off places, or indeed from any place other than one's own, while things like bananas and oranges were unknown to that whole generation of children. One had to hoard and manage very carefully to make something like a simple fruit cake. Clothing and fabrics of all kinds were severely rationed and coupons were saved with miserly caution in order to be able to buy one decent outfit, if one could find the like.

Probably the worst feature for most people was the petrol rationing. It was strictly controlled, and almost from the moment war was declared, all private cars were off the road. No petrol meant no petrol and we just had to grin and bear it. We had to resort to bicycles for most journeys, and we cycled fairly long distances. We thought nothing, for instance, of a journey to Knock from Bridgemount and back, almost forty miles, though not quite, for on bikes we took the short cuts on awful roads. It kept one beautifully fit, as gradually even distance seemed unimportant, but there was always the problem of weather. What we did for food on such missions, I cannot imagine – as there was little available in Knock on a week day we probably carried it with us in baskets and flasks, which added to the sense of adventure. On pilgrimage days, however, things were different, we needed to carry all sorts of things, food, milk, flowers, uniforms and other essentials for a long working day. Liam had an official petrol allowance to get to his courts, which was normal practice for some public officials, but that was barely adequate for its purpose, and had to be managed carefully. There was a chap in Belcarra village who had a car for hire, and every Sunday, and any other special day, he would come and take us to Knock and get us home in the evening. We had to keep him permanently booked, no doubt there were other clients who needed him from time to time, but he kept all of us mobile and satisfied, and seemed very happy to do so.

Despite all the restrictions, pilgrims managed somehow to come to Knock. Many walked, as they had always done, even from distant places, others used trains when they ran, as by that time there was hardly any coal for the engines, and the railways were using turf, which, more often than not, was wet, so getting to journey's end took time. Buses too, were severely restricted, but it seemed as if the difficulty in getting to the end of journeys became a challenge that had to be overcome, for get there they did.

A notice in the *Annual* for a Vigil on 14 August during one of those years makes interesting reading. Confessions were heard from 8 p.m. until 4.00 a.m. the following morning, the hour of the first Mass. Masses are then listed hourly inside the church, and at the shrine, or the gable, as it was then called, until 12.30 p.m. the hour of the last permitted Mass. In a report covering the night and day, we are told that nine thousand holy communions were given out at the early Masses, while twelve priests were in attendance for confessions through the night. I understand that during a recent Vigil – one of the regular monthly Vigils, which are held all through the summer months – well over fifty priests were present during the early part of the night to help with confessions and that has been the usual number all through the season. However, less than seven years after the foundation of the society to promote the Cause of Knock Shrine, we were already making progress.

8

Second book published
Knock Shrine Bureau in New York
Cardinal Griffin's visit
Fr Peyton

The war dragged on and finding transport became increasingly difficult for everybody. It was as if the country had returned to the days before cars, it was public transport or nothing. In some ways it was very pleasant, a sort of switch back to more leisurely times, but we had become used to cars by then. I had been driving for all of my adult life and it was difficult enough without them. During those years, despite the fact that numbers were, of necessity, reduced, several significant events took place at the shrine.

To open the pilgrimage season in May 1943, Dr Walsh, who by then had been appointed archbishop, formally consecrated the archdiocese to the Immaculate Heart of Mary. We had known Dr Walsh fairly well when he was president of St Jarlath's in Tuam and had frequently spoken to him about Knock, but naturally one wondered how he would respond to it, when as bishop, he became fully responsible for its development. However, during his years as archbishop we got to know him very well, and very soon realised that it was easy to approach him when advice became necessary, indeed several of the most important events in the development of the shrine took place during his time. As he consecrated the archdiocese that day, using the prayer that had been used by the Holy Father when he dedicated the world to Mary's Immaculate Heart at Fatima, it was reasonable to hope that one day Knock might be viewed as an equally significant shrine. The ceremonies were broadcast, and as usual, following every one of those broadcasts, we received numerous letters from people in hospitals, as well as from all over England and Scotland, expressing interest and appreciation of the work being done. Far more important to us at that time were the letters from those who remembered Knock from childhood, and sent us new and useful information about its early days. They also told us how delighted they were to hear that at last it seemed to be on the way to becoming a recognised place of pilgrimage.

So, as the new store of information on cures and other matters increased, Liam decided that the time had come for him to take a fresh look at his book, *Knock Shrine*. By that time also, several notable theologians had had time to assess the Apparition thoroughly and make an attempt to interpret its message. Arising out of this, it was possible to include an entirely new chapter on the message of Knock in the book. Senator Helena Concannon wrote a foreword, and we were able to include dozens of up to date pictures. In the spring of 1944 a completely new book, *Cnoc Mhuire in Picture and Story*, was published. The archbishop was very pleased with it, so much so, that he sent a copy to Rome, to the Holy Father. Before long this was graciously acknowledged by Pope Pius XII in a warm letter which carried a personal blessing for the archbishop, and a similar one for Liam. It was the first time we had a direct response from Rome to Knock and we were naturally very thrilled with it.

Later that year, we were approached by a Professor Pat Flood from New York, asking if we would co-operate with him in founding a sub-committee of our society there. After lengthy and testing correspondence, this was done. In due course, that sub-committee arranged that the new book be released by Liam under a new title, *Our Lady of Knock*, and published in an American edition which carried an *Imprimatur* from Cardinal Spellman. The book and all our shrine literature was made available at the Irish Book Store on Lexington Avenue, New York. We were delighted about all of this, as it meant that news of the shrine's development, and everything connected with it, would be readily available, not only to the thousands of Irish in that great city, but to anybody else who might be interested.

The following year the war ended, and as we had done at its beginning, so at its end we set about arranging as we had promised, a day of special prayer, a 'Thanksgiving Pilgrimage'. That took place in August that year, and once again, it was a huge event for its time. The sun shone from a clear blue sky as the pilgrims began to gather, and it was thrilling to watch them, if one could spare the time to do so. It was wonderful to realise that we had been spared from involvement in war, and to watch life returning to normal. The archbishop came from Tuam for the ceremonies, and Fr Angelus, OFM Cap, preached a stirring sermon. The shrine altar and the processional statue were banked with exquisite flowers which had to be specially ordered from Dublin for the occasion, there were no local florists in those days, so the flowers came down on the train the evening before and somebody collected them at Claremorris. The statue-bearers, who wore the now familiar blue and gold sashes for the first time, came from the thirty-two counties of Ireland. We had two hundred invalids, a huge number even today, enormous for those times. As I glance now at photographs of that day I am reminded of so many splendid young women who were then handmaids, and alas, are no longer with us. That day they stood in neat lines full of happiness and hope, wearing the first uniform we had, with its tight belt and a very crisp white veil, similar to a standard hospital uniform of the time. We replaced it very soon after that with our present one, which, as I have already explained, was designed with particular relevance to the Apparition.

A very special feature of that day also, was a set of splendid vestments which were worn for the first time. Some time before that, the Knock Shrine Society decided that special vestments for very special days should be purchased and presented by us to the shrine in thanksgiving for our country's safety. We looked at all the available vestments and all the catalogues of vestments, but none of them was quite what we had in mind. We wanted to find something that would be specially suited to Our Lady's shrine, and would reflect some aspects of the Apparition, but understandably, the like did not exist. In the end, we approached the Benedictine Sisters in Kylemore Abbey who were renowned for, among varied arts and crafts, their fine needlework, and we asked them if they might consider making them for us. They thought about it for a long time, while they established a fixed idea of the type of garments we had in mind, and the scale of the work involved. Then, to their great credit, they decided that they would take it on. They worked for a few years embroidering the yards and yards of rich pure silk with fine silken thread, work so delicate that much of it had to be done under a magnifying glass. When finished, the design incorporated symbols of the Apparition, interwoven with roses, lilies and golden stars. The garments were wide and full, very different from the old standard vestments then worn in Ireland. With their graceful lines flowing from the shoulder they were quite a novelty, and they turned out to be indeed a work of art.

All the time they were being made we were in constant communication with the sisters, getting a progress report so to speak, and when they were finished, the archbishop brought them himself from Kylemore to Knock to ensure their safety. They caused considerable interest at the time, and because of their unusual beauty, displaying the best of Irish design and workmanship, they received a huge amount of publicity. Times and fashions change, however, and a set of three pieces suitable for a High Mass then, would be no use at all today at Knock when dozens of sets of vestments are required regularly. At the time of the Holy Father's visit, it was necessary for the priests at the shrine to take a comprehensive look at the supply, and the white and blue vestments with the insignia of the golden rose, which were obtained for the chosen concelebrants that day, are the ones which are now mainly being used for ceremonies. The Kylemore vestments served their purpose well and were used frequently, until eventually they were no longer adequate, so they found a place in the new museum. Behind the making of those vestments there was one more long story in the history of Knock's development.

The following year, 1946 saw many things happen. We had our first visit from a cardinal, when Cardinal Griffin of Westminster, accompanied by his brother, Fr Basil Griffin, OSB, and the famous preacher of his day, Fr Vernon Johnson from Oxford came on pilgrimage. Possibly the highlight of that year was the first visit of Fr Peyton, the rosary priest. We had been hearing about Fr Peyton for some time, and had decided that he would be an ideal person to speak to the pilgrims. At that time, though still very young, he had achieved singular success in promoting devotion to the family rosary all over America, preaching, broadcasting, and enlisting the help of popular screen personalities from Hollywood to further his campaign. In doing this, he had become very famous in his line. After a great deal of negotiation, which was very difficult at that time – though not on the part of Fr Peyton – we managed to arrange for him to come. He came to us then, as a guest preacher with the Elphin diocesan pilgrimage, and large crowds heard him for the first time. The warmth and sincerity of his address touched the pilgrims deeply. At the end of his homily there was a tremendous response, as the thousands present burst into prolonged applause, the first time such a thing had happened at Knock. Over the years, Fr Peyton though becoming almost a household name in America, returned to us again and again attracting huge crowds every time, and he came almost to the time of his death when ill-health finally prevented him.

During that year also, Canon Grealy passed away from us, and with his passing, part of an era seemed to vanish. He had been parish priest at Knock since 1931 and we had worked with him closely since 1934. Though there had been times when that work had been difficult in the extreme for all concerned, we always recognised the fact that, whatever the difficulties we had to endure, he had the interests of the shrine foremost in his mind. It was on his invitation that Liam first wrote about Knock, and under his authority the Knock Shrine Society had been founded. During his time and with his co-operation, it was possible for the society to organise the erection of the gable oratory, the outside stations of the cross, and numerous other improvements to the shrine which were very necessary at the time. He was always involved in every pilgrimage, regardless of how taxing such activities must have been for him in his later years. He was part of the old Knock that we first knew and it was difficult adjusting to conditions without him. The days of the birettas and capes have long since gone; we are the losers, they added colour and charisma to their wearers, and seemed to endow them with an aura that was infinitely larger than life.

In that year too, we lost another great friend, Most Rev. Dr Morrisroe, bishop of Achonry. In those early days, when bishops did not readily come to Knock, Dr Morrisroe led his diocesan pilgrimage there every year. On his very first visit, he created a warm impression when he told the assembled priests and pilgrims that he owed his vocation to the priesthood to Our Lady of Knock, to whom his mother had prayed for that special favour while he was still a young boy. Each time he came, he made it his business to seek us out – wherever we happened to be working – talk to us, and to enquire about our progress in all things. He was genuinely interested in our work and always gave us tremendous encouragement, which meant a great deal to us.

As the summer days lengthened, and June became a splendour of sunshine, we had one of the saddest events of those early years when we lost our dear friend, Mrs Bridie Morrin. She had worked with us from the beginning, stood by us in all our difficulties, was there, a wise woman, to listen, evaluate and advise, her door was always open if we wanted to call on her for any reason, and her hospitality was boundless. She was also our first secretary to the handmaids, a post she held for several years, and which she carried out with meticulous care. Alongside this serious side to her character however, she had a wonderful sense of humour, and could see the funny side of difficult problems. When we were sent word about her death, which was more or less expected, as she had been ill for a little time, we were greatly saddened. We spoke to her relatives at some length, hearing about all the sad final things, but when all of that had been said, and I had time to collect my own thoughts, I could not help remembering all the fun we had had together on several occasions. One night in particular will always remain in my mind:

In the very early days we had the great privilege of having Fr Jarlath Ronayne, a Cistercian priest, come to stay with us. He and Canon Grealy were old friends, and some time before that the canon had invited him to come to Knock to preach. It was a great occasion, the first time a Cistercian had been allowed out of his monastery, whatever the reason, so it got a great deal of publicity. When, some years later, Fr Jarlath came again and stayed with us for a few days, the poor man was completely lost, as he was then an oldish man, trying his best to fit into a non-monastic lifestyle without causing us any undue trouble. Several times I heard him wandering quietly around the house in the small hours, unable to sleep or break the habit formed by the years of rising for nocturnal prayer. In those days of the all-night fast, he could not even make himself a drink or a cup of tea. He would then get up in the early, early dawn, preparing to say Mass, and trying to fill in the moments until it was time to go out, around 6.30 or 7.00 a.m., when there was a reasonable chance that somebody would be up and have the chapel open in Ballinafad.

Almost as soon as he came to us, we told him that if he would like to go anywhere special or wished to see any particular friends, we would be delighted to take him. By that time we had got to know all the surrounding beauty spots and places of interest very well, as we frequently took our guests to see them when the weather was fine. He thanked us and said that he would bear it in mind, and for a while we heard no more about it. Then one afternoon, he announced that he would, in fact, like to visit an old school friend, 'Little Jimmy Naughton in Ballina'. We were delighted that he had at last decided to make the most of his few free days, and we wondered how we might discover the identity of this fondly remembered stripling. We didn't have to wait very long for enlightenment, for we were soon told that 'Little Jimmy' was none other than the Lord Bishop of Killala, Most Rev. Dr James Naughton. A little taken aback, we suggested as diplomatically as we could that we should make an appointment, or at least telephone and say that we were coming, but Fr Jarlath would have none of it. All the fun, apparently, lay in the 'surprise' element, and in finding out if he would be recognised and remembered after all the years. There was absolutely nothing to be done about it, except to get on with it. As soon as I got a chance to do so, I got in touch with Mrs Morrin, as I knew that she and the bishop were old friends, in fact while he was still a young priest, he had married James and herself, so it was a friendship of long standing. I told her of our problem, wondering between ourselves if Fr Jarlath would even get in to see the bishop, and begged her to come with us. Never one to miss out on fun, she saw the potential in this situation, and immediately agreed to come along, so at the appointed time, we collected her in Kiltimagh and we set out for Ballina.

Fr Jarlath looked forward a great deal to the encounter, and spoke about nothing else on the way, telling us with great enthusiasm how he proposed to deal with it. We drove straight to the bishop's house and suggested to him that to make his surprise call effective, he should get out and just ring the doorbell, which he did. We had decided from the outset to let him negotiate the manoeuvre alone, so that we would not spoil any of his fun, but all the time we wondered how far he would get. By some miracle, however, he was admitted, and after a very, very long time, he came back to us beaming all over. It seemed that the visit had turned out to be every bit as good in reality as it had been in anticipation. Delighted with the success of this venture, and by now flushed with excitement, he then got the notion that as we were in Ballina, we might as well make the most of it, and make just one more call, again on another old friend, 'Little Anthony Timlin' in Crossmolina, which for some reason, he reckoned, was only round the corner. We waited a little anxiously for the identity of our next quarry to be revealed, and were not unduly surprised to discover that 'Little Anthony' was none other than Canon Anthony Timlin, who was then vicar general of the diocese!

By that time it was late afternoon and Crossmolina was

quite a drive over roads that were then absolutely appalling. I caught a glimpse of Mrs Morrin and as her eyes caught mine they opened wide and she raised them slowly to Heaven. Nevertheless, they twinkled at the prospect, and it was obvious that she would not have missed it for the world. Again we suggested a message, telegram or telephone, although I cannot imagine telephones being all that easy to come by in North Mayo in the 1930s, but even if we had found one, Fr Jarlath had his own ideas, it had to be a 'surprise' with no advance warning.

Prepared for the worst, we drove on to Crossmolina and straight to Canon Timlin's house, where again, this time without any prompting, Fr Jarlath got out of the car, almost ran to the door and rang the bell. The housekeeper came at once and said that the canon had just gone to the church, but that she would go and get him. Standing in the porch, Fr Jarlath spotted him through the window, just as he was about to go into the church, and he made off after him at high speed, his voluminous habit blowing behind him in the wind, leaving all of us to follow or not as we pleased. We watched him as he caught up with the canon, who, without a moment's hesitation, recognised him. Then with his arm around Fr Jarlath's shoulder, they re-traced their steps, and disappeared into the house, forgetting about us completely in the delight of the re-union. We made our way back to the car, very much amused by what we had seen. Our amusement, however, became somewhat pale, when, after what seemed to have been an extremely long time had passed with no sign of either of them. Eventually, remembering us, they both came rushing out, full of apologies, asking us to come in for something to eat, and no doubt make an evening of it. At that stage, however, we were only concerned about getting home, so we declined.

By then it was dark and the bog roads were still before

us on the way home; no words of mine could now describe those roads at night, no lights, virtually no sides, cats' eyes or markings, and practically no signposts or hazard warnings. Eventually, after a lot of further chat, we got Fr Jarlath, very reluctantly, into the car. It was an exciting journey back. It seems almost incredible now even to remember, for it was almost a link with a world long passed. Fr Jarlath had for so long been an enclosed priest that he had never been in a car at night, and it was a whole new experience for him. He couldn't figure out why the lights were at the front only, and kept marvelling at it all the way to Kiltimagh.

It was also very late and anticipating a late return, I had already told Mrs Morrin that we would not delay with her in Kiltimagh, but would come straight home to Bridgemount for supper. She, however, had other plans. When we arrived at Kiltimagh she invited Fr Jarlath and all of us in to have a 'bite to eat'. There was no holding him then. Of course he would come into her home and visit with her, an acceptance given with more than a touch of old world courtesy. From then on there was no point whatever in our trying to do anything else. In any event, we were by then all of us starving.

Mrs Morrin too, had forseen that such a situation might arise, and had arranged the whole thing with her housekeeper before she left, so we were escorted into the dining-room where places had been laid out for full supper, which was served to us without delay. At one end of the dining-room table there was a huge bowl of carefully arranged fresh fruit. I shall always remember Fr Jarlath as he spotted it, and running to the table he sat down, gathering the bowl in his arms with great gusto. He then looked at me with a great expression of mock sadness as he asked wistfully, 'Why have you never given me anything like this?' This of course, was part of his fun-loving nature. No doubt it would seem a childish incident by today's standards of behaviour, but in the light of the circumstances of that moment, it was very amusing. Indeed maybe in truth, such a bowl of fruit may have seemed an unimagined luxury after the years of frugal fare in the monastery. I suppose we finished supper sometime in the small hours and returned home tired but satisfied from our day of unconventional adventure. Mrs Morrin had always been a part of our early exploits. She was a charming vibrant lady, but above all else, a deeply spiritual person. Her loss to all of us, but particularly to me, was very great indeed.

On the whole, it had been a year of great losses, we lost people who had been with us from the beginning, people who had stood by us on all occasions. It was not easy to replace any of them, and in truth they never will be replaced, but in the extraordinary story of the development of the shrine, new people with new qualities, qualities relevant to newer times, were sent to us by Providence and, in turn, they contributed in their own special way the particular expertise which was then required.

Judy and her husband, Liam, before leaving for their honeymoon to Paris, 11 February 1924

In the garden at
Bridgemount,
c.1930

Judy with five of her sisters, c.1925. L–R: Nancy Joyce, Alice Lyster,
Judy Coyne, Peg Begley, Lilian Ronaldson, Marie McGrath

Judy (right) with her sister Peg, c.1922

Bridgemount – 'more and more through the years I have felt God's presence in its silence'

A quiet corner of the gardens at Bridgemount

Apparition Gable at Knock Church in 1935 when the Knock Shrine Society was founded

With the first handmaids, L–R: Mrs K. Houlihan, Miss E. Clarke, Miss M. Clarke, Mrs Coyne, Mrs K. Mullaghy, Mrs B. Morrin

Sick pilgrims with handmaids and stewards outside a 'temporary' first aid centre in the early 1960s

Judy Coyne and Mr P. Molloy, Vice President of the Knock Shrine Society, holding the Knock Shrine Banner in St Peter's, Rome, after it had been blessed by Pope Pius XII.

9

Post war conditions
New buildings
Holy Year trip to Rome
Archdeacon Cavanagh research
Liam's death

As supplies of all commodities and transport generally
improved in the years immediately following the war,
the number of invalids coming to the shrine continued to
grow. We soon found our cramped conditions in the huts
inside the north gate totally inadequate, and it was becoming almost impossible to deal with the sick. By that
time we had a new parish priest who had a very different
attitude from Canon Grealy's, so getting any new facilities
was a major problem. However, after lengthy negotiation,
and a great deal of manoeuvering, we finally got permission
from the archbishop to erect a 'temporary' building for invalids – all our buildings were 'temporary' in those days –
on the south side of the grounds, a little to the north of
where St Joseph's stands today. It was given to us on condition that all fittings would be portable, but by that time
we had grown accustomed to the insecure nature of our
tenure and we were very pleased to get it. It neared completion as we came close to our Day of Recollection; it was
to be of course, our only base, as the original huts had been
dismantled. But it seemed as if there was no hope whatever
of its being finished, and in the end, having got tired of
negatives on all sides, I went to see the builder myself. He
told me that he was having problems with finishing the roof
as he was finding it next to impossible to get the extra

roofers required. I put it to him that if I could get him extra workers to help, he would finish it in time; he agreed reluctantly, but he was certain that I would not be able to find them. In the end, with the assistance of Mrs Hoban, a handmaid from Claremorris, I got in touch with a reputedly competent man, who, when I went to talk with him, remembered that he had once done some work for my father. Those were the days of loyalty and that was quite enough to tip the balance in my favour. As a result, he made himself available, promising to bring along extra men. It was an answer to our prayers as the building was finished, the roof going on the night before our big day.

Again, it was almost entirely a wooden hut, with a corrugated iron roof. It had a kitchen, a couple of 'wards', which were no more than two wooden divisions, one for men and another for women. It had toilets and dining-rooms for handmaids and stewards as well as for the sick. We had a covered way where we could store invalid chairs, and the luxury of some cupboards where blankets could be locked away. It may sound substantial as described, but it was absolutely basic, providing no more than the bare necessities, without even a hint of comfort. It was little more than a shelter where we could give essential care to the sick, and there it ended. We could not have known it then, but it became the background for many important events, and it was to house us for almost fifteen years until we moved into a completely new era of development.

Around that time we were dealing with the rosary devotion which Fr Peyton had introduced a short time before, and we were publishing our Rosary Calendar, which was then given to members as a sort of enrolment token, but in recent years we had to discontinue because of high printing costs. We had decided on a particular picture for the cover of the next edition, but as our only copy was not at all clear,

I asked Liam one day when on his way to a court in Castlebar, if he would take the picture to a photographer there, to see if he could make the definition a bit sharper on a new negative for printing. He took it with him, and talked with the photographer about our requirements, which seemed to be reasonable. Then he arranged to collect it a couple of days later, on his way back from a court in Westport. When he got home on that evening however, he hadn't got the photograph. Apparently a scratch was appearing on the negative each time it was made and the photographer could do nothing to clear it. Never one to give up on anything I had decided to do, I set out for Castlebar myself and called on the photographer. He seemed to be defeated by the picture as he told me he had made several attempts to get a good negative, and he actually showed me copies pinned up in his studio, all with a noticeable scratch. Undeterred, I asked him to have just one more try, while I went to the church to pray for his success.

He glanced at me quizzically and, with a smile, said that it would appear to be a case of 'bell, book and candle' but he promised to try again. I said that I would go and pray while he worked on it and that he should pray too. I did as planned, giving him plenty of time to deal with the new negative then I returned to the studio. This time he was triumphant, and showed me a perfect specimen without a trace of a scratch. I asked him how he had managed to do it, and he replied that he didn't know, as he had treated it exactly the same as the others. There was no further difficulty then in getting on with making the print. I thanked him and asked him if he would perhaps come to Knock to take pictures for a movie film of the children's pilgrimage which was scheduled for the following Sunday, and this he agreed to do.

As it happened, the day of the children's pilgrimage

turned out to be a positive deluge; we were up to the ankles in mud and water, with an accompanying storm which made conditions miserable for all concerned. Our photographer turned up as promised, and did all he could to take good pictures, in fact he did splendidly, producing work that captured the spirit of the day – quite an achievement in any conditions. We already knew that he had been an engineer who had retired early on health grounds, and he had come from the north of England to live in Castlebar. He got great pleasure from fishing, something that is easy enough to do in the numerous little lakes and rivers which are so close to the town. He had taken up photography professionally, and by then was making quite a success of it. He was not, however, a Catholic, though he appeared to be very interested in Knock. Soon after that he told us that he had watched the children that day on pilgrimage and concluded that a religion which could attract children and adults in such conditions, must have something special to offer. In due course he told us that he was having instructions in the Friary in Ballyhaunis and, after a time, he invited Liam and me to be his sponsors at baptism, a task we took on with great pleasure.

That story however, had a strange ending, for almost immediately after his baptism he went to Cork one day to collect mounts for pictures he had done for us. We had tried to discourage him in this, as we said that Cork and back was too much of a drive for one day, and so he decided to spend a night there. Somewhere on his rounds in Cork he met a friend from Castlebar quite by accident, and since petrol was still scarce, and since this friend had not brought his car, the photographer offered him a lift home, an offer which was instantly accepted.

On their way home later that day they stopped for a meal in Ennis, but suddenly he became ill, so ill in fact, that he had to be rushed to hospital, where they pronounced his condition to be critical. It was more than that, it was a full scale emergency. By strange coincidence the sister who was in charge of him in the Ennis hospital had nursed for some years in Castlebar and remembered him, so knowing that he was not a Catholic, there was no question of calling a priest. However, his passenger, who was of course still with him, and very anxious about his condition, told her of his change of faith and a priest was quickly called. By an even greater coincidence, the priest who came to answer that call had led the pilgrimage from Ennis to Knock the previous Sunday, so he was truly among friends. He gave him the last rites without delay and, almost at once, the photographer died.

We had planned to take him and his wife to lunch the following day in Kylemore Abbey, where the nuns then ran a guest house, to mark his reception into the Church. They had themselves chosen the venue from various options we had given them and were looking forward very much to seeing Kylemore, while we had organised with the nuns to give them a very special celebration meal. When we got in from Mass that morning the phone rang, and we thought of him at once, deciding that he was calling us in good time to let us know the exact time he would be ready to set out, but instead of a celebration lunch, we had to go to Ennis to his funeral. When finally the full story emerged, it was realised that he had received five of the seven sacraments of the Church within as many weeks. It looked like a singular miracle of grace.

Sometime late in 1949, the Pope announced that the following year, 1950, would be a Holy Year. We felt that we, the society, should do something special to mark it, and following many hours of discussion among the council members, we decided that we should do the obvious thing and arrange for a pilgrimage of handmaids and stewards to go to

Rome. Going abroad then was a big adventure, it was still some years before the advent of mass travel and so planes were a novelty to most people. However, at a very early stage in the planning we decided against going overland, which was the usual route, and we put all the arrangements in the hands of a steward who was a local travel agent. Very quickly and very efficiently, he laid on two planes, which we filled without any difficulty, and in early October of that year we all set off from Dublin airport, then known as Collinstown. We made a stop-over at Paris to visit some of the shrines in the area, and then we flew on to Rome. Such arrangements today would be quite out of the question for most people as it would work out to be so very expensive.

It was a very crowded week, trying to do the impossible, see Rome and everything in it in a few days, but we fitted in as much as we could and most of the handmaids and stewards who travelled with us enjoyed it very much indeed and thought it to be well worth while. We had an audience with the Pope, then Pius XII, in Castel Gandalfo, and we had places in St Peter's for the beatification of the foundress of the Sisters of St Joseph of Cluny. However, because of poor organisation on the part of the people on-site, to whom we had delegated responsibility for this important part of the pilgrimage, it very nearly didn't happen. As soon as we arrived in Rome we were told that we would have to be satisfied with places in the square, despite our requests of almost a year before, and above all, the assurances from them that everything had been looked after. Knowing that all who had come with us would be so disappointed, having been already told that arrangements had been made, Liam and I did our best to get something done about it, but we were promptly told that nothing whatever could be done at that stage, and anyway that was 'not how things were done in Rome'. Not being particularly impressed by the 'When in

Rome' argument, we immediately thought about Monsignor O'Flaherty. We had already written to Monsignor O'Flaherty to tell him we were coming to Rome, and as he had told us years before that he would do anything he could for us when we came there, we were somewhat surprised that we had had no reply. On making enquiries about his whereabouts soon after our arrival, we were terribly disappointed when told that he was away and had been away for some time, hence his silence, but there we had to let the matter rest.

During dinner on the night before the beatification ceremonies, Dr Waldron from Ballyhaunis who was also in Rome and staying at another hotel, called in to talk to somebody in our party. Almost by acccident, though I don't think it was, I overheard him speaking at the next table and telling of his wonderful day, and all kinds of wonderful things, and special places he had seen, under the guidance of Monsignor O'Flaherty. On hearing this we exchanged glances, and spoke with Dr Waldron, asking him if he was sure of all he was telling, as we had been told that Monsignor O'Flaherty was out of Rome. He replied that, yes, he had been, but he was now back and he had spent the day with him. We literally bolted from the hotel to find a taxi to take us to the monsignor's office. By some absolute miracle we found him at home; he had only returned to base that morning. He was delighted to see us and anxious to hear all the news from Knock. However, we lost no time in telling him about our immediate problem, though naturally, he was not at all sure at that point if he could help.

On his suggestion, we went with him to the relevant office and, having found it, were told by the young monsignor who was dealing with tickets that as far as he could remember, they had all been distributed ages before, and there were none left. Never one to be put off easily, Monsignor O'Flaherty asked him to open the drawer which had contained the tickets and have a good search round, which he did. Monsignor O'Flaherty then leaned over and pulled the drawer out completely tipping it upside down as he did so, while one ticket fell out, then another, and another. At that point he turned and asked us how many we were, while he counted out enough for our whole party, plus two over. It was an incredible turn around and it was wonderful to be able to go back to the hotel with enough tickets for everybody and a couple to spare. He had given us two tickets for very special places, and these we gave to our priests, Dean Daly from Claremorris, and Fr Malone from Knock, the spare ones we were pleased to give to two students who were staying at our hotel and were most anxious to be present. I am quite sure that nobody in the whole of Rome, other than Monsignor O'Flaherty, could, or would, have done the like. As it turned out, it was a wonderful opportunity for us to see St Peter's decorated in all its splendour for the celebrations, something we were to experience again in later years, but with ourselves then very much in the forefront. It turned out to be an interesting week, but the great moment for Knock in Rome was still in the future.

During 1952, we were becoming increasingly aware of the significance of Archdeacon Cavanagh in the history of the Apparition. When the material for the first book was being collected, we gradually came to recognise the major part he had played in the Knock story. The importance of that part, because of lack of time during the initial researches, had not been fully analysed and needed to be given closer investigation. He had been parish priest at Knock at the time of the Apparition, and had earned the reputation of being a singularly holy man. Numerous theories had been put forward by learned theologians about the reasons why Knock had been singled out for this special manifestation, yet all of them had overlooked the legendary sanctity of the parish priest. At the time of the Apparition, he had just completed a sequence of one hundred Masses for the Holy Souls, an unprecedented act of charity, undertaken on his own initiative, as nobody better than he had understood the simple fact that his parishioners were then too poor to have Masses offered for their dead. It was commonly believed by the people of the parish, including some of those who had seen the Apparition, that Our Lady had appeared to the archdeacon on several occasions in his cottage which stood close to the chapel wall. In such circumstances, her reported presence at the gable that night might not have seemed all that extraordinary. Yet, he was not among the witnesses. Priests who were his contemporaries and who remembered him, including Canon Grealy who was a clerical student at the time, singled him out as a man of extraordinary sanctity. Gradually, as the picture became clearer he emerged as a man apart, one worthy of further study.

Nothing much had been written about him, contemporary newspapers gave accounts by experienced newsmen of his singular devotion to the Mother of God, and of his great humility. On these aspects of his personality they had written in striking terms, in fact through all the accounts these singular qualities clearly emerged with striking unanimity. Journalists are not by nature people who give credence to stories unless they are reasonably satisfied with their authenticity. Their accounts then, were the sum total of the written word, but there were still some people alive who remembered him. It was a question that continued to nag at us, to be dismissed and put to the back of the mind, but on every occasion, it returned to the surface. It was a situation when something had to be done, and done quickly, while the subject was still clear in living memory. We talked about the archdeacon a great deal around that time, and one day we decided that his life and history should be systematically investigated. Liam phoned the archbishop, Dr Walsh, and made an appointment to see him, and once again we went to Tuam to talk to him. At the end of a very long discussion, which examined all relevant aspects of the the man, the archbishop suggested to Liam that he should try to do something about assembling whatever material could be found and putting it into a book. Liam returned from Tuam that evening wondering to himself and to me how he might go about it, and inevitably blaming himself for having brought it up at all, but he knew quite well that it was one more task that had to be done.

At that stage he was coping with very heavy official work, while at the same time his responsibilities at the shrine had become very demanding indeed. However, he managed to do a little research most days. When he returned from court and finished his meal, he would take up his notes or his typewriter and work at the manuscript for as long as possible. All through that winter and into the spring he worked steadily, trying to contact people who might be in a position to give him authoritative information and, as luck would have it, mostly succeeding. It was extraordinary how the memories of that very saintly priest had been cherished by so many people who were crucial to the enquiry.

Eventually, the task was finished and the manuscript was sent to the archbishop for the final *Imprimatur*. We then asked Cardinal Dalton, who had also known the archdeacon and was known to have admired him greatly, if he would write a foreword to the book, and this he did most willingly and without delay. The manuscript, however, remained in Tuam for what appeared to be a very long time, with no word about it from anybody, and for a while we even forgot about it. Then one day, Liam began to wonder what had happened to it. The more he thought about it, the more convinced he became that the archbishop had decided that it should not be published. I, however, couldn't imagine such a thing to be possible in view of all the discussions and the positive decision that had been taken about it, so, taking the initiative myself, I decided to phone the archbishop and ask him what was happening. I put a call through to Tuam – in those days one had to call on the help of an operator to be connected – and got through at once. The archbishop answered the phone himself, he was full of good spirits and praise for the manuscript which, by coincidence, he said he had just posted back to us. He also told me that it would require no revision whatever, and it could be printed off at once, which was very good news. It was published very soon afterwards, in May 1953. Since then, because of ongoing demand, and a new awareness of the importance of Archdeacon Cavanagh in the history of Knock, it has run to many editions, and is still in print.

The spring and summer of 1953 saw the season come, and then slowly drift to a close. An announcement was made by Pope Pius XII that the following year would be a 'Marian Year'. This was something quite new to us, but then it was new to everybody, and we wondered what arrangements would be made for Marian shrines to mark the occasion, and if our own Marian shrine would be considered to be one of them. In view of the general attitude to Knock at the time, we decided that it would be ignored. However, at that stage, I don't suppose anybody gave the matter very much thought, we certainly didn't, as we didn't really know what might be involved and we had just been through a very heavy and demanding year in every sense of the word.

On 2 September, Liam returned from a court in Castlebar and, having dealt with the urgent mail, I remembered that I had several things to do at Knock. The season was drawing to an end and there would be another big day on the eighth, so I decided to go over and get down to the left-over work, and put things in order as far as I could. Liam decided that he would come with me, but on that particular evening, I tried to discourage him, as the court had been a long one and I knew that he was tired. However, he had made up his mind that he was coming and as my sister Peg was staying with us at the time, she came along too. Peg and I did whatever we needed to do, while Liam went into the church and prayed. When we had finished our various bits and pieces, we set out for home.

Almost as soon as we had left Knock, Liam, out of a thought, brought up the question of our involvement there, and with an apparent sadness in his voice, he wondered why we were keeping it up. There we were, he said, over twenty years from the time we first became interested yet, as he saw it, very little had been achieved. We were satisfied that through our efforts the number of pilgrims had increased, and a general interest in the Apparition had been re-kindled, yet in his view little of real consequence had been accomplished. All three of us talked about this and, for a while that evening, we seriously wondered if we should drop the whole thing at that point. We felt that the people who really mattered to the work had no interest in it, in particular those on whose support one should, in other circumstances, have been able to count. All of this had apparently been weighing on his mind as a few days before that, after a court in Newport, he had called as he usually did, on his sister in the Convent of Mercy there, and apparently had voiced the same feelings to her. Sr Patrick heard him out and said to him that one could do only one's best in all things and trust in God to do the rest. This feeling of despondency must have been very strong, and the conversation with Sr Patrick very important to him, as on his return that night, he told me about it. Then, on that long remembered journey back from Knock, I reminded him of her advice and this seemed to cheer him a little. We agreed that we could do no more than our best and resolved to continue to ask Our Lady to help us. We knew that for the moment we could do no more and, satisfied in that knowledge, we began to say our rosary and no more was said.

We all went to bed at our normal hour and, as far as I know, neither of us gave any further thoughts to our doubts, I certainly didn't, as there was a good deal of work ahead of me. I suppose it had been one of those bleak moments that beset people now and then, sometimes before things change for the better, though in my case that was certainly not so. Very early next morning, sometime before six, just as the hazy September dawn was breaking, I woke and realised at once that Liam was not well. The previous year he had had a problem with his heart, but he had recovered, his specialist had certified him fit for work and he was working normally. At that stage, no longer seriously ill, he had been put under the care of the local doctor, who had examined him only a few days before and told us that he was, in fact, very fit, news which cheered us both greatly. Now, however, I knew that he was gravely ill, in fact I think I recognised the inevitable. I ran to Peg's room and woke her, then I chased downstairs and roused Pat, asking him to go quickly to Ballinafad and get a priest – in those days the telephone service went off at night. Neither of them could believe me, but they both came instantly and Pat did as I asked. I went back to Liam, but in a very short time, it was all over, he died just as the clock was ringing to wake us for Mass.

I remember very little of what happened for the rest of the morning, who in such circumstances can? As soon as the priest and doctor had left us and the stark realisation of what had happened was beginning to dawn, Peg began the long ordeal of trying to contact members of our two families, or at least the main ones, who would tell the others.

She managed to reach all of them before the one o'clock news from Radio Éireann carried the announcement of his death and put an end to private grief. The next few days came and went; I, unable to grasp what had happened to me, or to realise that life as I had known it would be no more.

It takes a long long time to understand fully the bleak reality of separation and bereavement. I suppose most people spend days and months almost in a trance, doing things automatically, unaware of the total desolation that has overtaken them. I know that up to a point, I did. On the day of the funeral at Knock, when Mass and all the sad rituals were over, John Jordan and Paddy Molloy, two very kind and considerate stewards and, as I was to discover in the years that were to follow, two very staunch friends, spoke to my sisters, Marie and Peg, who were then both staying with me, and asked them to make quite sure that I would come to Knock on the following Sunday. To do otherwise they said, would be very unwise, and as a result I might never come again. Perhaps they knew more than they were prepared to say, or perhaps their intervention was again purely Providential, that I shall never know.

The following Saturday came as every other Saturday through so many years had come, preparing for the Sunday and the pilgrimage, and yet, on that occasion, how different! Peg and Marie wondered together how they might get me to go to Knock as usual, and they finally decided to speak to me about it, though they had more or less concluded that I would not be able to face it. Somewhere in my subconscious however, I was aware that I would now have to carry on, absolutely on my own. I don't know how much constructive thought I gave to the matter, very little I should think, constructive thought is not normally part of bereavement, but somehow I managed to compose myself, at least outwardly, and just hold on. For that particular moment, no more seemed to be necessary. I also knew full well that I had to go to Knock. I had to go there, there my work would be henceforth. In the end, there was no need for anybody to try to convince me. I went to Knock that Sunday, and I went the following Sunday, and I went again, and continued to go as usual, gradually realising that my way forward from then on would be very much on my own. I was young enough then to have done otherwise, several people change course at a much later stage, but bit by bit I realised that I must continue to devote my every effort to Knock. I prayed a great deal, I was greatly distressed; Liam and I had been blessed with great happiness and our whole life together had been one of total sharing. The prospect of going on without him was almost impossible to contemplate, yet, thanks be to God and to His Blessed Mother, I was given the grace to be able to deal with sorrow and I fully realise that without that grace I could not possibly have done it.

The autumn days passed slowly and sadly, I must admit that off and on I contemplated the future with anxiety and some fear. Very soon it would be Christmas, and before long it would be a new season, which I would have to tackle alone. The archbishop, Dr Walsh, was very concerned for me and was full of kindness. He offered to get me a priest to help me, or at least, a secretary, but such things were not to be. It was a winter and a spring that I would rather not think or speak about. Yet, the ways of the Lord are truly wonderful. I did not then realise that the first truly meaningful era in the history of our work for Knock was about to dawn, and my one regret when those wonderful things began to happen, was that Liam was not there to see them, and to share the joy they brought. In retrospect however, and with the benefit of many years' experience, I am quite certain that he was helping me and guiding my hand. Before all that was to happen, however, there were some in-cidents concerning my work for Knock which were painful in the extreme. However, crushing though they were, they were probably necessary, as they revealed to me a determi-nation and strength within myself until then unknown, a determination which had never been necessary to call upon in all the years that had gone before, but on which I had to rely again and again, and, as it happened, was to be my salvation on many occasions in the years that were to follow.

10

Bereavement
Triumphant pilgrimage to Rome
First meaningful recognition for Knock

No doubt people remember some phases in their lives more than others, there are periods one tends to recall with pleasure, and others which are best forgotten. In my case, the autumn of 1953 and the whole of 1954 will always be with me, though for very different reasons. As the autumn days following Liam's death grew darker, and the winter nights closed in around me, I was aware of my total loneliness. I missed his vibrant personality around the house and the close companionship which was so much a part of our years together. I had been married at nineteen and during all those years I had been sheltered and protected from all sorts of problems. No longer having a man of substance at my side, I was very soon to learn how difficult it could be for a woman to hold her own in what was then, and I rather fear may still be, very much a man's world. Almost at once I was made to realise my new status when I had to take some very firm stands and come to terms with difficult situations far sooner than the period of compassion normally granted to grief dictated.

The work continued all through the winter and I did the best I could to cope with it. The personal worries were also there and the cold reality of having to do everything alone, with nobody to consult, was an enormous strain. The stream of letters grew and there were numerous meetings to attend, all of which gave me plenty to think about and left me little time for self-pity. In the circumstances, that was a good thing and, though I did not recognise it as such, it was exactly what I needed then.

One day, as I was about to go to a meeting in Dublin, having planned to travel up on the midday train, I picked up the letters which had just been delivered and, selecting those that seemed to be most urgent, I took them with me and left the house. I was staying overnight in town, so Pat Burke drove me to Balla station, where the train stopped in those days, and there I caught it. Having settled myself in the carriage I began to open the mail. Among the letters was one from Jim Finn, a Roscommon steward, who was also a teacher. In it he told me that a young priest, a former pupil of his, had written to him from Rome, saying that 1954 had been declared a Marian Year and there would be a particular focus on Marian shrines all over the world. All of them, with the exception of Knock, had already had special talks given about them on Vatican Radio, and as this priest was considering the possibility of doing such a talk, and knowing that Jim was involved in working there, he had written to him asking for some information about it. Jim enclosed the priest's letter, and asked me if I would write to him direct, as he had already contacted him and said that he was asking me to do so.

On my return from Dublin I sat down and wrote to the priest, sending him our various publications and saying how delighted we would all be to know that Knock might be spoken about on Vatican Radio. I knew nothing about the priest at the time, but he turned out to be Fr Dominic Conway, later to be bishop of Elphin, who was, in all the years that followed, a true friend to Knock and particularly to me. I got a reply very quickly, Fr Conway was obviously very interested in the project, and soon a very fruitful correspondence about Knock began between us. From those letters I came to understand the full significance of the

Marian Year, and its singular importance in relation to Marian shrines. Liam and I had discussed it from the time it was announced, but at that time there seemed to be little regarding Knock that we could do about it. Now I began to get the idea that we should arrange a special pilgrimage of handmaids and stewards to Rome when our Knock season had finished, which would coincide with the end of the Marian Year. I put this idea to our council when we had our next meeting, and they felt that as representatives of Ireland's Marian shrine, we should certainly be there.

I then got in touch with the archbishop to talk to him about it and, having made an appointment, drove to Tuam to see him and told him of our idea of visiting Rome. At that stage, he was reluctant to give us much encouragement, and thought that perhaps somebody in Rome, perhaps Fr Conway, could represent us, but it was obvious that he was not particularly keen on the suggestion. It may indeed have been due to kindness on his part, as he was well aware that I was desperately trying to find my feet at the time. However, I was not prepared to let it go at that, particularly as the days passed and I became increasingly convinced that we should go.

Meantime, Fr Conway came home. His mother had not been well, and she had by then become a patient in Ballinamore – a nursing home near Kiltimagh, run by the St John of God Sisters – where he came to visit her. He also came here to lunch on a couple of occasions, and we talked about the proposed trip, for which no concrete arrangements had yet been made. He was most encouraging about everything, and he promised that he would find out all about the official plans for the ending of the Marian Year as soon as he got back to Rome, and would let me know about it as quickly as he could. Very shortly after that he returned to Rome, but when some time had passed and I had heard nothing from him, I began to wonder what had happened to him, and to all the information he had promised to send me. The days passed, the summer seemed to be almost drawing to a close and it appeared to me that nothing would come of the plans for Rome.

One day when I was putting flowers on the statue in the invalids' building, a priest came along and began to chat. In those days people frequently wanted to find out more information about the shrine, and handmaids always stopped whatever they were doing to give that information if they possibly could. We spoke about various things and, before long I discovered that he too was based in Rome. He was a Dominican, a Fr David Sheerin, whose sister was a handmaid. We talked a lot about the developments and plans for the future and he seemed to be very impressed by all he had seen. He ended up by promising to write an article for the *Annual*, which in due course he did. During our conversation I mentioned our idea for a pilgrimage and also Fr Conway's interest. He told me that he knew Fr Conway, and he promised to track him down on his return to Rome, try to discover something about the official plans that were being made and, between them, send me all the information they could find. That seemed fair enough, but I was well aware that time was getting short.

However, having returned to Rome he could not have known that Fr Conway had been taken ill on his long hot drive back and was then recovering in hospital somewhere in the mountains. Unable to find tidings of him from anybody, he went himself to the Vatican to try to discover something about arrangements, but he had forgotten that it was still holiday time, with almost everybody out of the city on holiday. However, with the help of a young monsignor who had been holding the fort in the relevant office, they managed to find, at the bottom of a drawer, a single copy of the document telling about the declaration of a new feast, the Queenship of Mary, which was to be celebrated on 1 November and, apparently, was to be the highlight and the official end of the Marian Year. He was told that copies of that document had been sent to every country some time before, and he had stumbled over the last one. True to his word, Fr Sheerin wrote to me at once, sending me that single copy. When I had read it and realised the importance of the ceremonies which were being organised in Rome, I phoned the archbishop straight away and asked him if I could come to see him.

We made an appointment for later that afternoon; I went to Tuam and I took the document with me. The archbishop read it through very carefully, then, without any hesitation, he agreed that we must go to Rome. I asked him if he would come with us, but at that point, he declined, though later he decided to come. He then told me that I would have to make all the arrangements. This was a new and unexpected responsibility and I was at a loss to know what to say. I told him that I didn't know even where to begin on such a venture, but he laughed heartily at me and, rummaging in his desk, gave me a scrap of paper with the telephone number of a firm in Liverpool, where he said I could book a plane.

It was long before the days of booking planes from Aer Lingus, Ryanair, or anybody else, and that telephone number was my only lead just then to our getting there. Without wasting too much time, however, I picked up courage as soon as I got home and did as the archbishop suggested. Sure enough, the firm existed, they had planes for hire and we were in business. That plane provided the stewards who were with us with endless entertainment on the way out, as they invented imaginary holes in the floor for the benefit of the more faint-hearted amongst us. Flying was still a new experience for most of us, and for sure there was real anxiety among some. I don't suppose our aircraft was the latest model jet by any means, far from it, it was pretty basic, but it got us there and home again without any undue worry.

Fr Conway was then attached to the Irish College in Rome and, having recovered and returned to his base, he wrote to me as soon as he possibly could explaining the delay. He confirmed everything that Fr Sheerin had told me and added a great deal more. Then, at the request of Dr Walsh, who recognised the value of the help he was already giving us, Fr Conway made all the arrangements for us while we were in Rome. These local arrangements are the making or breaking of every pilgrimage, or holiday. Indeed, they are the principal ones; if properly carried out then everything goes smoothly and everybody is satisfied, if not, then one is left with disappointed and disgruntled travellers. Fr Conway's involvement was an enormous help to all of us, much more I am sure, than he ever realised. He spoke Italian fluently, knew all the worthwhile places of interest for us to visit, and saw to it that we got there. It seemed to us that he possessed a secret code of access to every inner sanctum in the city and, what was more important, as those doors opened to him it was obvious that he was very well known and always very welcome.

At a very early stage in the arrangements, while we were in the corresponding stage, he told me that there would be a very important procession from the Basilica of St Mary Major to St Peter's for the crowning of the picure of Our Lady, a picture which is called 'Salus Populi Romani'. I was later to learn that this ancient picture which is housed in the Borghese Chapel in St Mary Major, was greatly loved by the Romans, as traditionally it is believed that it once saved their city in a time of plague. It was to have a place of very great honour in the celebrations of the new feast, when all the principal Marian shrines in the world would be represented by a special group of people walking in the procession, each group carrying their own banner. He said that we should be in Rome for that procession with our banner. Now that was a new problem for us, we did not have a banner at Knock, there had never been a need for one, and so it was a question of having one made. I looked around and wondered where the like could be done, it was not going to be easy and time was not on our side.

In the end, I went to Bernard MacDonagh in Sligo, who was then rapidly becoming a well known artist, and I talked to him about it. Wonderful to relate, he painted a picture of the Apparition on one side of a canvas, with Our Lady of Knock on the other, and we were well on the way to having something to show. While the picture was being painted, I took its measurements and all details to the Franciscan Sisters in Loughglynn, who had taken on the job of mounting the canvas. I explained to the sister who was to carry out the work that we wished to have the picture framed and bound with royal blue Foxford flannel, a fabric which had been chosen to match sashes of the same colour and material being worn by the stewards. She was horrified at the idea, as she thought flannel to be the most unsuitable material imaginable for the job; satin, yes, velvet, yes, but flannel, never. She had a point of course, aesthetically it would probably have been a great deal more beautiful mounted in either, but we were determined to give it an Irish flavour and, after considerable reasoning, I managed to get her to agree. When it was finished, she was the first to say that it looked very well. Like everything connected with that pilgrimage, the banner was delivered at the eleventh hour, but it arrived. Then, there was the unexpected but real problem of the supporting poles which were long, very long, indeed at the crucial moment we feared that they could not get them on to the plane, but they did, and it all came together.

We took off from Dublin airport, then a very small complex, and in order to give those who were with us good value for their money, we had scheduled a stop at Lourdes. We paid our respects there and then, very early next morning – it had to be early as our schedule was tight – and in a torrential downpour, we left for Rome, arriving at Ciampino airport just as the Angelus bells were ringing out all over the city. Fr Conway was at the airport to meet us with our own special bus, or coach as it would be called today, a bus which took us everywhere during the whole of our visit, and we all set off for our hotel. There was not much time to spare or to relax however, as that evening we were due to walk in the procession which was to mark the beginning of the ceremonies.

When we had rested a little and changed into our uniforms, we gathered in the Basilica of St Mary Major, as arranged. It was a solemn occasion, but even so it was not without its lighter moments. Long before we set out for Rome I had written to all the handmaids who were going, about the importance of having very presentable uniforms, and in particular, good white shoes. Senator Costello who was coming with us, and who was never one to take directions lightly, had bought herself a new pair of high-heeled white shoes. Though then in her eighties, despite diplomatic entreaties from me, she set out undaunted to walk the long miles, and in fairness, she trotted along with the best of us. I don't remember that she came to any harm from the experience, though she probably suffered silently.

As we set out on our long walk in the procession which followed the flower-framed picture of Our Lady, we were greeted by thunderous applause from the thousands of Romans who had gathered to watch. As we progressed along each street, and our banner came into view of more and still more people, this clapping seemed to grow in volume. By the time we got to St Peter's and yet more people had gathered to watch, it became a thunder. We were told that it was the first time women had walked in procession through Rome, but I don't know how true that was. As we walked, every street along the way presented a new vista of colour, there were flowers and lights adorning little private individual shrines of Our Lady all along the route. Thousands of flags hung motionless in the still air, while the hundreds of balconies were draped with rich tapestries, their colours resplendent in the gold of the evening sunlight. All the time, the bells of the city churches pealed out, mingling with the voices of the pilgrims who sang hymns and prayed. The Romans certainly gave their picture, and us, a wonderful and a noisy welcome. Night was falling as we reached our destination and, exhausted though we were, we were completely thrilled when we entered the vast Basilica of St Peter, which by that time was entirely bathed in light. Soon even more lights were switched on, and in a positive blaze from floodlights and flashing cameras, the picture was carried inside and placed on the altar to await its solemn crowning next day. We then returned to our hotel; by that time we were all tired and starving, but very happy.

Sometime after dinner that night, word was sent to me officially, that out of the four hundred banners representing the numerous Marian shrines all around the world, twenty had been selected for a special blessing at the ceremonies next day, and among that twenty would be ours, the Knock banner. It was almost incredible and I chased around quickly to tell the others. At the same time, I had also been told that I would be called on to present it, and I should be ready to do so. It was, however, a banner which needed two people to carry it so, as Paddy Molloy, who was vice-president of our society was with us, he was the obvious person to escort me, and this decision delighted him greatly. The rest of the evening was spent by both handmaids and stewards making sure that our uniforms were freshly pressed, shoes and white gloves were spotless, and everything ready for the big day. We had all been exhausted before dinner, but on hearing this news, we got fresh life and some of us talked about it for hours, unwilling to go to bed or to bring the day to an end.

Next day, Monday 1 November, was one I shall always remember. The sun shone brilliantly from an early hour illuminating the ancient city with that soft hazy light which is peculiar to Rome. It was going to be a perfect day for the crowning ceremony, the climax to the Marian Year. We made our way to St Peter's, where Mass was to be celebrated at 10 a.m. in the presence of cardinals, archbishops, bishops, hundreds of priests, diplomats and pilgrims from every country, including our own. Moments before the appointed time, the Holy Father, Pope Pius XII was carried into the Basilica where, in a positive explosion of light, he ascended the Throne to begin the ceremony. Then came the moment for which we had all waited and, as arranged, we were given the signal to go forward, the first banner to lead them out, so to speak.

As we carried it to the papal throne, the solemnity of the occasion did not deter the Romans and the vast international congregation from bursting into thunderous applause as they greeted the banner from Ireland. 'Irlanda', 'Irlanda' they yelled, again and again, 'Viva Irlanda'. We were aware of the cheering on all sides of us and tried to realise that our own banner from Knock, poor Knock, a joke for so many, many, years, was now among the chosen few, there at the very heart of Christendom to be greeted and blessed by the Pope himself, a vindication, had we needed one, of all those troubled years. It was a moment which those of us who had lived through the development of Knock till then were anxious to savour to the full and remember for ever. We knelt as we were presented to His Holiness, who blessed us, and sent his special greeting to our families and friends. Then, scarcely believing what had happened to us, and full of pride and gratitude, we returned to our places amid still more cheering. The special medal which the Holy Father had given us reminded us however, that it was indeed true and it had not all been a dream. The climax for everybody was the crowning of the picture with twin crowns which, wrought from purest gold and sparkling with jewels, were placed on the twin images of the Virgin and Child. Cameras flashed as photographers from the world's press recorded the moment. It had been a tremendous experience, and a wonderful beginning to our stay in Rome.

When the ceremonies were over, something told me that I should get a photograph of that magnificent crown. I don't quite know why I had that notion, but I had, and I asked Fr Paddy McAllister, later Very Rev. Canon McAllister, of Belfast, who was with us, and who was a brother of one of our handmaids, Rosa, where I might find the like. He thought that I should have no problem finding one and so I set off on my own looking for the picture in all the souvenir shops around the Vatican. They didn't have any, but one of them volunteered the information that all such official pictures were taken by the Pope's personal photographers and could be obtained from their studio only, the studio of Felici on the Via del Babuino. Relieved to know that I had not been on a complete wild goose chase, I went back to the hotel, found Fr McAllister who had not yet left, and told him of my searches. He looked at the address which I had scribbled on a piece of paper – having been a student in Rome, he knew the city well – and he knew that this studio was quite a distance from where we were. In the circumstances, he suggested that he would come with me as I did not know Rome very well, and we called a taxi. We found the studio without any difficulty, but as it was still only a few hours since the ceremonies, understandably, pictures were not available, so I ordered and paid for copies to be sent to me at home. Then, quite satisfied with our day's work, we returned to the hotel.

That evening, we all attended a reception at the Irish College, as guests of the rector, Monsignor Herlihy, and with us he welcomed the archbishop, also the archbishop of Dublin, who was in Rome for the occasion, as well as Dr Finbar Ryan, archbishop of Trinidad. That evening also I met Fr Garde, provincial of the Dominican Order, among the guests. Inevitably we got talking about Knock. He had never heard of it until that day and was most impressed by all I had to tell him. Arising out of that meeting he came on pilgrimage to the shrine, within a few weeks in fact, and he organised the first Dominican pilgrimage there on the second Sunday in October the following year, a date the Dominicans have held as their own for their annual pilgrimage ever since.

The following few days were particularly memorable and included so many notable events that it would be difficult to single out any one for special mention. The archbishop said Mass for us in the catacombs, which was very interesting to those who had not visited them before, indeed it was special for all of us. During the whole length of our stay in Rome, he was entirely relaxed and full of fun, enjoying every moment of it with the rest of us. We visited the principal places of interest, always with Fr Conway to shepherd us, and to explain many things to us which we would otherwise have missed. Our special bus waited at the door of the hotel to take us to whatever place was scheduled for that day, and in the evenings, the sightseeing done, it got us safely home again. We had an audience with the Pope at Castel Gandalfo, where we were received and singled out once again with gracious welcomes and cheers, as extra special visitors. One very unusual outing was a visit to the Campo Santo Lorenzo on All Souls' Day. A visit to a cemetary would not normally be very high on one's list of places to visit when sightseeing abroad, yet the suggestion could have been made only by somebody with very great sensibility, as that visit in Italy, on that particular day, was a rich experience, full of sunshine, of flowers and of joy.

I think joy would have been the perfect word to describe that whole pilgrimage. Everything about it from the beginning to the end was full of joy. The handmaids and stewards who came with us were singularly light-hearted, and in our free moments, indeed in some serious moments too, they found plenty to laugh and joke about. Our hotel, the Columbus, on the Via della Concilliazione, was splendid, of top international standard, and situated as near as we could have got to St Peter's, which made a tremendous difference to us. All that said, however, I don't think I got one wink of sleep during our whole stay and that was difficult to understand: our hotel was entirely satisfactory, the food was excellent, the beds comfortable, and the rooms spacious, restful and elegant. I was exhausted at the end of each day, which should have guaranteed sleep, but the responsibility for the whole undertaking was mine alone, and I was very conscious of the fact, so I could not relax, not even for a single moment. All things considered, however, the whole thing worked out so well that in the end, I made up my mind that I would never again return to Rome. Any other visit, I decided, would be an anti-climax. I went with the others to the Trevi Fountain, but I don't think I was among those throwing in a coin. Just as well that we don't know of things in advance, because it was by no means an end to my encounters with Rome.

At the end of our visit, we were very sorry indeed to have to leave, Rome is a city which has so much to offer to so many different people. However, we were very grateful to God that everything had gone so well for us, everything connected with our pilgrimage had been successful beyond our wildest dreams. On the morning of our departure our bus collected us at our hotel for the last time while we, almost too sad to speak, boarded, and were soon rolling back towards the airport and our plane. It had been a memorable week, on that fact we were all quite satisfied.

In all the excitement that surrounded us, nobody had told us that the papers and the news bulletins at home had been following our every move. Radio Éireann, in association with Vatican Radio had broadcast the ceremonies of the crowning, with a full commentary in English telling everybody in great detail about what was happening, and of the tumultous reception given to the Knock contingent. The station had stayed live on air for several hours that day, so that people at home had been made very much aware of our visit, and of Knock and its significance, yet again.

I returned home after all of that elation and joy to what was to me an empty house. Though Pat Burke had been the watchful custodian in my absence, and though my sisters Marie and Peg who were with me in Rome, came back with me, it was still, as far as I was concerned, an empty house. Liam, the one person with whom I could have shared the realisation of all that joy and savoured with him its full significance, was no longer there to hear of it, and I had to do all my reminiscing, probably the best part of any happy experience, alone. It was very difficult trying to come to terms with the sadness of that particular occasion, but somehow, thank God, I got the strength to do so. I managed at last to get some very overdue sleep, as I was totally exhausted, but my resting hours were to be short. The letters had piled up in my absence and the Rome trip was rapidly generating a whole batch of new ones, so there was nothing more to be done but settle down quickly to work.

11

Announcement of crowning of statue
Bringing crown to Knock
Personalities involved

I was beginning to get myself more or less organised after my return from Rome and had recovered somewhat from all the excitement, when I had a call one morning from the archbishop. His voice sounded bright and cheerful, as he told me that he had good news which he wanted me to be the first to hear. The moment he began to speak I guessed what the news was going to be, but even so, it came as a great surprise. He went on to say that he had just had a letter from the Vatican, in that morning's post in fact, informing him that they were granting permission to crown our processional statue with full ceremonial. This was something we had been asking the archbishop to do for for quite some time and though he had never actually refused, it had always been put on the long finger. He then said that he hoped we could settle on 8 December, the official end to the Marian Year in Ireland, to do this. Following so soon on the presentation of the medal in Rome, it seemed like a singular turn of fortune for the shrine, and I found it difficult to realise that at last, so much seemed to be happening, and happening all at once. He then said that we must use the existing crown for this occasion, as there would be no time to do otherwise. That soon re-collected my thoughts and focused them at once on the collection of gold and jewels which we had assembled over the years – gifts from the people of Ireland for that specific purpose. I knew full well that those people would be very disappointed if the crown to which they had so generously given was not after all, available and ready. I reminded the archbishop about this and he assured me that he had not forgotten, but as there was not sufficient time to get the special crown made, we would have to make do with the one we had.

Once again it seemed to me, Providence was guiding my steps, as that morning also I had received in the post the photograph I had ordered of the Roman crown, gold for which had been collected in very similar circumstances and which would, I was convinced, be a superb model for us. I told the archbishop about this, a development which at that moment seemed to be more than coincidence. He was very interested to hear that I had got the picture, as he too had thought that particular crown magnificent, yet he was quite positive that such an intricate piece of work couldn't possibly be completed in the short time at our disposal. He also felt that if it were rushed, it might well be ruined. However, I asked him to let me try. The gold and the jewels were already with the goldsmiths – they had been for some time, as we had had some sacred vessels made already, by then it had become almost an ongoing programme. I suggested that I phone Alwright and Marshall, the goldsmiths we had been using for several years, to discuss the project and send them the picture in that day's post so that they could decide if it could be attempted. These jewellers had been chosen by the archbishop himself and had been entirely satisfactory at every stage, so I asked him if they could take it on, would I have his permission to commission it. To this he readily agreed and said that there was no harm in asking, and even if it could not be ready for the official day, we could use it on future occasions.

As soon as I had finished speaking to the archbishop, and put the telephone back in place, I calculated the number of days before the eighth. There were not many, and it didn't look at all promising. In all honesty I had to admit to myself that it seemed to be out of the question. However, I breathed a silent prayer and dialled the number. Mr Alwright answered the phone; he and his wife ran the firm and they employed a small staff of specialist jewellers. Mrs Alwright was a very helpful lady, who had a great interest in Knock and in the work we were doing. She also had a very artistic flair and was always ready to discuss design and its possibilities with us. Just then, they were in fact working on the Cross of Cong monstrance for us. Over the years, we had been collecting gold and jewels for it as well as for the crown, and by that time we had assembled a very fine collection for both. Before they commenced work on that monstrance, however, we had had great trouble deciding on an acceptable design and it was discussed regularly by members of our council. We were very conscious of the fact that people would be most anxious to see the finished piece, as we had been gathering material for it for so long.

One day, during that time of indecision, when visiting Dr and Mrs Costello in Tuam we happened to talk about the monstrance yet again. There was a picture of the original cross hanging in the Costello's drawing-room and, out of a thought, Mrs Costello, glancing at it quite by accident, casually remarked, 'Why not that?' I stopped and considered the suggestion, and at once replied, 'Why not, indeed!' It was a model we had never thought about, and yet at that moment, we knew that we had found the answer. Cong was so near to Knock, and here before us was a picture of that ancient artefact, magnificently wrought, one of our national treasures, the ideal choice for a Mayo shrine. Dr Costello, who was very familiar with its history filled us in on its every artistic and historical detail, but we knew even before he expanded on it, that we could do no better. We asked Mrs Costello if she would come with us to the archbishop to discuss it, which she did, and arising out of that, the design was finalised. There were problems, however, about its execution, as the original was a traditional cross, possibly a processional device, and our monstrance had to have a stand on which it would rest for Exposition and Benediction of the Blessed Sacrament. This was something that had proved difficult to solve at the time, and the archbishop was not happy about any solution which had been put forward up to then, since as well as the practicalities, the stand had to be aesthetically acceptable.

As it happened we were in Dublin one day around that time, and it suddenly struck us that we should ask the people in the museum for their advice. They, above all others, we reckoned, should know about antique design and might provide an answer to the problem. Without wasting any time we phoned and explained our difficulty, and it says much for them, that without any undue fuss we were able to make an appointment almost at once. We went along to the museum where we met Dr Joseph Raftery, who was then Keeper of Antiquities. We talked to him about our difficulty, and he very kindly offered to get one of the museum's design experts, their graphic artist, Eileen Johnston, to discuss it with us. She came along to talk with us and, as well as being a very courteous and charming lady, she was obviously a very efficient artist who understood at once what was required. After a very short explanation, she offered to make a model for us, and in what seemed to be no time at all, she sent it to us. On its receipt, we took it to the archbishop, and from that point on there were no further difficulties.

All of that was in the past now and the work was going ahead on the monstrance, but suddenly the question of a crown was emerging and taking the form of an urgent priority. Mr Alwright had known of the plans for it for quite some time, but in the long period of indecision, he had not,

I am quite sure, ever imagined that it would turn out suddenly to be a matter of such urgency.

He thought about my request for a minute or two, then he said that he couldn't promise anything until he had seen the picture, the reaction I had expected, but at least he had not said no. Next morning, soon after I got home from Mass, he phoned me to say that they had received my note and the photograph, and had studied it; it was going to be a very big challenge, but they were prepared to have a go and see how they might get on. I phoned the archbishop to tell him that they were going to attempt it and, like myself, he did not hold out much hope that it could be done, and advised me strongly to think about an alternative.

When I had time to consider the complexity of the work I thought it even more impossible. The design for the 'Salus Populi' crown was very intricate. Fashioned from pure gold, graceful spirals rose from a fine circlet to several points and fell back again to form a series of pointed arcs, each arc encasing a cluster of finely set jewels, while still more jewels were set on top of each point and around the forehead band. The work was delicate and required a high degree of very specialised skills. The Knock crown which was to be similar, had some modifications apart from those required for size and fitting. I certainly did not realise then that my request was going to be the cause of having several jewellers working twenty-four hours a day, but even if I had, I imagine that I would have had the same reaction: It was going to be a very privileged occasion for the shrine, and it was up to everybody concerned to do everything possible to make that ceremony, and everything connected with it, a truly fitting tribute.

The days that followed were hectic in the extreme. I was in constant touch with the key members of our council, they were my main support in those days, and they were always ready with helpful and welcome suggestions. I was slow to phone the jewellers, but now and then I did, and was assured all along of good progress, although I didn't dare hope that the work would be finished in time. I was becoming reconciled to the fact that we might, after all, have to use the old crown, when one morning Mr Alwright called me and said that the new one would be ready on the evening of 7 December. I could hardly believe what I was hearing as, though I did not dare admit it even to myself, it seemed that it could not possibly be done. I was, of course, absolutely delighted, for in all my anticipation and enthusiasm, I had not really counted on its completion and, for once, had made no real plans to receive it.

Suddenly I woke up to the fact that we would have to get our precious crown from Dublin to Knock on that particular evening, and the realisation of that fact at that late hour in the proceedings almost resulted in a state of panic for me. I phoned one of our Dublin stewards, Larry Cusack, who was a practical businessman, and told him of our difficulty. He, however, could see none, and offered to collect the parcel himself, and get it to Knock the moment it was ready. Somewhere at the back of my mind, I remembered that he drove a good car and that was a first requirement, but at the same time, I was also becoming increasingly aware of the responsibility and the real danger for any person alone of trying to guard this precious parcel, even in those relatively peaceful days. I said this to him and between us we decided that it would not be a very wise thing to undertake. We then remembered Diarmaid Fawsitt, who also lived in Dublin, and who was very much to the forefront on the Dublin-Knock scene at the time. Diarmaid's family had been connected with the legal profession for a very long time, his father and brothers being very well-known members of the judiciary. I can't remember how we first met, he probably came on some Dublin pilgrimage and got talking to us, but when we got to know him better, he would breeze down to us occasionally, always ready for fun and always in good form. On that occasion, he seemed to be the ideal man for that particular mission, so I contacted him and, as expected, he was very enthusiastic about the whole affair. It seemed to appeal to his sense of adventure and he had all sorts of gallant plans for it. In the end we decided that both he and Larry should be couriers for the evening.

At the appointed time they went to the jewellers, but they had to wait, all that intricate tracery had taken far longer to complete than expected. They waited and waited, as the minutes lengthened to hours, and there was still no sign of the crown. Eventually, it was ready, and they were handed their precious parcel. As it was then very late, reason should have told them either to go home or, since Diarmaid then lived quite a distance from town, to some hotel for the night, but they had given their word, and to Knock they were going. So they set out, fully aware that the cold December night was getting colder and that a storm was rising. The Dublin-Knock road would not be very inviting for a midnight escapade even now in very bad winter weather, but in those days it would, at some points, have been a positive nightmare. However, having prayed fervently for a safe journey, they drove on, and after several anxious hours driving in appalling conditions, they reached Knock. Then well into the small hours, but knowing that they were expected, they drove straight to the presbytery, where I don't suppose they were made very welcome, but they delivered the crown. Their difficult mission for the night had been well and safely carried out; exhausted and hungry, they set off to an hotel in Kiltimagh for what was left of the night and to take refuge from what was by that time, a raging gale.

Many times afterwards they told us of that midnight odyssey, and of their very real anxiety through the night about the whole assignment. It was not, of course, without its funny side. Fully appreciating the possible dangers of their undertaking, although they would never have admitted the like at the time, partly for fun, but still with a little concern, they had bought themselves a truncheon: a sort of shillelagh, heavily ornamented with shamrocks and harps, something intended as a souvenir for tourists. I would not care to be at the receiving end of a blow from it however, as despite its folksy appearance, it is indeed very heavy. On a subsequent visit to Bridgemount, Diarmaid gave it to me as a memento of the night, and it rests on a bookshelf in the study to this day.

Next morning, 8 December dawned, bringing one of the worst storms we had ever experienced. It seemed to us on getting up as if nobody would be able to get to Knock that day, and that our well-planned crowning ceremony would have to be abandoned. Trees had fallen on all sides and heavy snow was beginning to come down. Peg and I, together with Pat, prepared to set out for Knock almost as soon as it was light, or what was taken for light. Pat, who sometimes drove the car, took one look at the conditions and decided and that we would all be quite mad to venture out. However, as I saw it, it was going to be a very important day and weather was not going to stop me without at least a try. It was still early morning and, hoping it might improve, I took on the driving. Pat, knowing that he would be needed during the day, if we ever got there, decided that he had to come; it was good to know that he was with us and could take over if the worst came to the worst. When we got very near to Knock village on the Claremorris side, almost at the top of the hill a tree had fallen across the road blocking it completely. In the prevailing conditions there seemed to be little hope of its being cleared for several hours, so I turned and went back, heading across roads which, even in good weather, were little better than boreens, and that morning were almost impassable. Beside and behind me in the car Peg and Pat were joining me in fervent prayer that we would make it, while I plodded on for what seemed to have been hours. Our Lady must have listened to us, for we got to Knock without further incidents. By that time the whole place was covered in several inches of snow, which was drifting rapidly, so the prospect for the day seemed singularly bleak.

The crowning ceremony was fixed for the afternoon. Who in their senses would make arrangements for any fixture in early December in the west? We really wondered if anybody at all would be able to make the journey. All through the morning we worked feverishly, giving the final touches to the statue to adorn it fittingly for its crowning. It was standing in the old invalids' building which, even in high summer was bleak and on that December morning was bitterly cold, with an icy wind blowing through the cracks in the door. However, the cold was the least of our worries. As various stewards came and went collecting their bits and pieces, we asked each one of them for the latest weather report, fearing the inevitable answer, as conditions grew steadily worse.

We dressed Our Lady in a gown of pure white silk, woven with silver tissue, and on her head we placed a veil, delicate as gossamer. Some days before, I had sent an order to a florist in Dublin for flowers and they had sent them the previous evening on the train. We fixed the flowers on the carrier and, when it was finished, it was a beautiful sight, the feathery white petals of the chrysanthemums peeping through the lacy green fern soft as the falling snowflakes. Then there was the problem of getting the statue over to the church in that raging storm. In the end, we covered it firmly in strong plastic sheeting and pinned the sheets securely in place. Four stewards then carried it to the church while we walked beside them, struggling to hold ourselves erect in the gale and praying that it would not be blown to tatters. The stewards, however, got it to the church without the slightest damage. Though it was then almost dark and still blowing a bitter biting wind laced with sharp particles of snow, we found that the church was packed with pilgrims with almost as many outside who could not get in. Before long, the archbishop arrived and the crowning ceremony began.

On the very first word from the archbishop, the intensity of the storm cut off the electricity and extinguished all the lights in the church and all over the village. We were left in almost complete darkness, except for the feeble glow from a few flickering candles. I prayed, and no doubt everybody else did too, that light be restored. Undeterred, the archbishop continued with the ceremony by candlelight. Then, just as the crown was being placed on Our Lady's head, some engineer at some point, managed to reconnect power and the lights came back on, revealing the full beauty of the golden crown glittering with its precious jewels. The hushed silence of that moment will stay forever in the minds of the many who witnessed it. One of the priests then asked the people if they could clear the centre aisle, so that the statue could be taken down through the church for all to see. Slowly, they managed to move, there was nowhere to go other than out into the night, there was no further room. Just at that moment, from the back of the church came the high-pitched trembling voice of a very old lady as she called out slowly yet very clearly, 'Hail, Holy Queen, Mother of Mercy', and at once, the whole congregation joined with her quite spontaneously in the familiar words, words learned from the lips of parents and grand-parents, a salutation, a welcome and a prayer. It was a glorious moment; the people had come from north, south and east Mayo, from Galway, Roscommon, Sligo and Connemara, the country people who through the years had kept the flickering flame of devotion to Knock alive. They had come again to share in the joy of that evening and to bid a welcome to their Mother with natural west of Ireland grace.

The ceremonies over, the pilgrims then made their way to the buses and their cars. Newspaper reports next day tell of the scenes of devastation that awaited them on their return journeys: roads flooded, bridges swept away; the train returning to Dublin, which had several of our Dublin handmaids on board, had to be abandoned at Athlone, while buses took the pilgrims on by diverse routes. They reached home in the small hours, many, including a handmaid, Mary Fagan, to find their houses flooded, and having to find accommodation elsewhere for the night. Dublin too had taken a battering in the storm. Earlier in the day, General Seán MacEoin, one of our stewards, then Minister for Justice, with Mrs MacEoin, a handmaid, and his driver, had to be rescued from his car, when they had run suddenly into severe flooding en route to Knock. One newspaper man who managed to get through told us of seeing in his mirror, a bridge collapse behind him a moment after he had driven across. Miraculously, he got to us safely.

For the first official honour that was bestowed from Rome directly on Knock, the heavens were not exactly 'telling the Glory of the Lord', it seemed to us rather more like a chorus from hell.

The following summer for the anniversary of the Apparition, which is the main feast day for Knock, we were singularly delighted, after the long years of waiting, to have the processional statue with its magnificent crown used in procession for the first time. As it so happened, the weather that day was beautiful, soft and warm, with a clear blue sky. It was a great thrill to watch the procession as it set out down through the village, which was the custom in those days – it had to be, there was nowhere else for it to go, and whatever through traffic there might have been had to wait patiently until it was all over.

As usual, for such events, we used the best flowers that could be got and prepared the statue and its stand with more than usual care. Immediately behind it, two government ministers, who were vice-presidents of the society and also stewards, Mr Joe Blowick, Minister for Lands, and General Seán MacEoin, Minister for Justice, carried the banner which had been blessed by the Pope. It was one of those rare days when at last everything seemed to be just perfect, and we were able to realise, if only for a very short time, that we seemed to be making some progress.

I had a great deal of work to do following the crowning ceremony, and the inevitable follow-up to the Rome trip, most of which I had put to one side to deal with the crowning and all that it had entailed. Christmas was also approaching, and between one thing and another, I had little time to think about myself or my personal difficulties. I was gradually coming to terms with the fact that I now had to do everything on my own. True, I had splendid handmaids and stewards, a first class council, men and women who had courage and were prepared to speak out and make their feelings known, if they felt such a course was necessary. Nevertheless, I knew that they looked to me to make most of the plans. It was difficult, there is no doubt about that, and there were times when I almost didn't succeed.

However, it is essential that one should remember the good times as well as the difficult ones. During that period I received great kindness from the handmaids and stewards, who seemed to sense my sadness and quietly came to comfort me in so many ways, often sending me Mass cards or chocolates. They were little things individually, but they meant a great deal to me then when every kind thought made such a difference. There was John Jordan and his wife Breege who inspired me with so much courage. By that time, John had become chief steward, full of ideas and vigour, and their kindness and encouragement when they came to help me at Knock was boundless. They frequently came to the house to visit me also, always to try to cheer me, to make a favourable report on progress, and point out to me the good side of things, always adding their own special refreshing humour.

Many people will still remember Paddy Molloy and his wife, Kay. One could depend one's life on Paddy, kind and considerate gentleman that he was. One or other, and sometimes both of them, would phone me on the day before a bank holiday, telling me that they would be calling for me at a certain time the following day. Knowing that there was no post delivered or collected on bank holidays, they would not listen to any excuses on my part, or heed my usual protests. At the appointed hour they would call and take me to the sea, or to the mountains for a few hours, and afterwards on to an hotel for a meal. All of that was most helpful and therapeutic, getting me away from worries and routines, and allowing me to forget responsibilities even for a few hours. Kay was a very artistic person, who loved nature, and her delight in the open spaces and the beautiful scenery all around us was wonderful to share. She particularly loved Lough Gill and during those visits we got to know the lake and its surroundings in its every mood and every colour. Indeed in all the times I have seen it since, even to today, it continues to draw up for me clear memories of those times. Kay wrote some charming poetry about those beautiful places and simple pleasures, sensitive and delicate verses as she shared her joy with us. God rest all of them, they were real friends when I needed them most, their kindness and concern helped me greatly in my re-adjustment during that, the most difficult period of my life.

St Joseph's, handmaids old and new

Now and then it is necessary to go back in time to put the present in perspective and so I must go back to the 1940s, when we had a telephone call one day from a handmaid who lived in Belfast, Dr Patricia McGee. I cannot remember the precise date, as so much was happening at the time and claiming attention. She said that she wanted to see us both, Liam and I, very urgently and she would come down to Knock at the earliest possible moment to talk to us. I had known Patricia for some time then, she had been a handmaid for a few years and was a niece of Dr Mageean, the bishop of Down and Connor, whom we had met on that Lourdes pilgrimage several years before. I first met her quite by accident when she had come to Knock on a pilgrimage from Belfast and she happened to hear me speak to a group of pilgrims about the Apparition. She came to me afterwards to make further enquiries, especially about the handmaids whom she had seen that day for the first time. She and her husband were both doctors running a busy practice in Belfast and soon after that, she became a handmaid. During her spells of duty, periods she had to fit in as her professional work permitted, she would stay either with us here in Bridgemount, or in St Mary's hostel, depending on which of us could accommodate her at the time. On that particular occasion, however, she went to Knock and we went to meet her there.

By that time her husband had died and she was busy picking up the pieces and getting herself together again. She told us that on the day she had phoned us she had come in from a busy morning surgery and had begun to tackle the ironing; her children were quite young at the time so she had little time to spare. In the midst of her ironing her thoughts drifted to the handmaids, and the organisation generally, and it occurred to her that, as a body, we seemed to be doing nothing about our continuity and stabilising our organisation for those who would take over from us in later years. Above all else, she thought that without some permanent headquarters in Knock, it would be difficult to ensure continuity.

Off and on during the years before we had ourselves thought about our continuity, but being still a relatively new establishment, it did not seem to be very urgent at the time. Having listened to Patricia however, and to her reasoned suggestions, we had to admit that what she was saying was true. She was also of the opinion that some few handmaids among us should make a permanent commitment to stay at Knock. It all sounded most logical and reasonable, but on reflection, who was there amongst us who would be prepared to take on such a task? Most of us were married, several others had good jobs which they were not likely to leave, and the young single girls would almost certainly marry, so the chances of finding such people seemed to be remote. We saw the wisdom in all of her suggestions, and we talked about the possibilities for the whole evening, but at that time there was little prospect of such a plan coming to anything. It was difficult enough to do the bare necessities in those days, never mind a major project for permanent handmaids at Knock. Such an organisation would also need a house of some kind, and as our sole claim to permanence then was a wooden hut, the idea seemed unrealistic.

Independent of Patricia's thoughts, however, we had been thinking for some time about the sick people who lived long distances from the shrine, who could never come

there because there was no place for them to stay overnight. This was particularly true of people with limited
means who could not afford to pay even a small amount for
accommodation. The Dublin handmaids had also asked us
many times if something could be done about this problem,
but at that time there was no obvious solution. We had
thought that perhaps in the future it would be possible to
build a simple hostel where the sick could spend a night or
two, with trained people to look after them. We had discussed those thoughts very generally with the archbishop at
one stage, but all such notions were put aside as there were
other impotant things taking every minute of our time.

Very shortly after Liam's death, I happened to glance
one day at the *Western People*, one of our local papers, and
saw an advertisement for a house for sale in Knock village.
Almost on impulse, certainly without giving it any serious
consideration I cut the advert out of the paper and, writing
a short note, posted it to the archbishop. In that note I
suggested that as the house was so near to the presbytery, it
should be considered for purchase, as either the house or
the site might come in useful for something, and in any
event, it should be bought, if only to prevent its use for
something that might in time turn out to be unsuitable for
that particular location. I was trying to deal with everything on my own at that stage, so there was no time for
thinking any more about it. On receipt of my letter the
archbishop passed it over to Fr Malone, who was then Administrator at the shrine, and asked him to purchase the
house, but nothing happened for some time, as Fr Malone
had some difficulty in clearing the title and tying up the
legal formalities.

I had more or less forgotten about it when I had a letter
one day from the archbishop, telling me that the purchase
of the house had been completed. The letter went on to say

that we could now have the house for the sick, and he asked me if I had any plans for its use. This came as a complete jolt to me, as I hadn't imagined that any immediate action might be required from us. However, there it was in black and white, a house being handed over to us, the Knock Shrine Society, so something had to be done, and done very quickly. I had no ready-made group of handmaids on whom I could call to equip and staff a house and was very uncertain about what to do. It is strange at times how one embarks on a project without quite knowing where it might lead and, on that occasion, I had no means of knowing how this particular venture might turn out. I certainly prayed, and I prayed plenty, and all the time I wondered where I might find the helpers who were so urgently needed, but there were no obvious answers.

I then remembered Mary Gillespie, who was, I knew, nursing with the Sisters of St John of God in Ballinamore. She was one of our handmaids, and a splendid nurse, full of life, good spirits and practical good sense. Without wasting any time I drove over to Ballinamore and talked to Mary about my idea. I was well aware of the importance of the decision I was asking her to take were she to become involved. I said as much to her, also that I did not want to influnce her in any way. She heard me out, and then, quite understandably, she told me that she didn't think it would be wise to give up her well paid, satisfactory and secure job, for something unpaid, and indeed something she might not enjoy doing. Even more important was the consideration that the Knock house might not even continue. Disappointed, but not at all surprised, I left her and drove home, trying to figure out where I might now turn to get the help we so badly needed. I should have had more faith in God and in his Blessed Mother, as had I known it, a solution was about to present itself.

One evening shortly after that, Mary and a few of the other handmaids came to Bridgemount for a meal. It was a beautiful summer evening, and when supper was over we decided to go over to Ballintubber Abbey, which was then being restored by Fr Egan and is only a short drive. Ballintubber has always been a great refuge for me, not always for the expected reasons, though I dearly love the place, but now and then with more devious motives. It is always an interesting place to take guests, but I must confess that on some of those calm evenings of summer, in the days before we had electricity when, because of that stillness, a solid fuel cooker was not pulling properly and it was quite impossible to produce a meal at the expected time, it was sometimes suggested that the guests be taken to visit Ballintubber, thus giving us that extra hour to coax the wretched cooker along.

On that occasion, however, nothing untoward had happened, and we went there with light hearts. We did the customary tour of the abbey, I marvelling as I always do at its unique serenity and peace and, having said some prayers together, we came back home. Before she left Bridgemount that evening, Mary took me aside when she got an opportunity to do so and whispered to me that over the past few days she had been thinking about all I had to say, and she had decided to come into our new house. She was quite definite, and not prepared to discuss it as she said she had made plans to do it right away. It was difficult to believe what I was hearing, but it was obvious that her mind was made up. Knowing that it was important to get things started, I lost no time in getting in contact with Fr Concannon, who had just been appointed Administrator at Knock, and I told him that it looked as if we would be able to go ahead as planned.

Fr Concannon was a very sympathetic and kindly man,

who had a great interest in the Apparition, and was very concerned about promoting the devotion in every way possible. Also, it was very easy to work with him. He was delighted to hear the news and seemed as pleased as we were to know that the handmaids would be in Knock permanently. Very soon after that, Mary and I went to look over the house and to see what we would require to equip it. As part of the sale, we had acquired some of the furniture already in the house, so that, at least, was a beginning. Almost as soon as Mary had made up her mind to come to St Joseph's, and word about the new house began to spread among the handmaids, we had an application from another handmaid, Kay Flynn, and before long, she too, came. Kay was a splendid cook, and for several years her presence made a very big difference to the easy running of St Joseph's. In another little while, they were joined by Delia Moynihan, who was a nurse and she too was a big help to Mary.

Later still Margaret Donnelly offered her services. Margaret had been a handmaid for several years and she was waiting on in her job until she could apply for, and claim, early retirement. It was not very common in those days, but she was hopeful of early release and was then looking seriously to Knock, She had been with the post office all her life, almost a founding figure of the post office in Ireland; in fact, she was the first post mistress to be appointed. She came to us then from her last position, in Castleblaney, not all that far from her home town of Clogher, Co. Tyrone. Margaret was a wonderful organiser of whatever she touched, were it in office or kitchen, and she gave sterling service from the late 1950s until her death in 1985. People still come to us to enquire about her, as she made a great impression on all who knew her.

During those years I had been going regularly to meetings in Belfast where, apart from Dr Patricia McGee, we had another splendid handmaid, Rosa McAllister. Rosa was a sister of Fr McAllister who was with us in Rome in 1954 and later president of St Malachy's College. I had been to Rosa's home on a few occasions; it was a large house in the Belfast suburbs and it was filled with rare antiques and beautiful things. Rosa was surrounded by every comfort, she had a good housekeeper, and a maid to wait at table. She bought her clothes from top designers and wore the best things she could find. All told, she was well protected from any hardship and life should have been very easy and comfortable for her, but, being a deeply spiritual soul, she put little value on any of those things. She decided to sell her house and come to Knock. When she told me of her notion I did my best to discourage her, as I knew both sides of the story, and I was only too conscious of the very big sacrifice she was contemplating, and the very small comforts we would be able to offer her. However, Rosa's mind was made up, and soon she too arrived to do whatever she could to help. She was a kind and gentle lady full of holiness, and she must have brought a lot of consolation and hope to those fortunate enough to have known her.

Some people may still remember the old St Joseph's as we eventually called it. It was a smallish modern house standing on the Claremorris side of the presbytery and set back a little from the road. It had a tea-room on the ground floor, so that meant there was one large room downstairs. After a lot of discussion, we decided to convert this into a ward, cordoning off a section for a smallish chapel, and at the other end, a bathroom, kitchen, toilets, etc. That was almost all of the downstairs accommodation, the bedrooms, such as they were, were upstairs, and they were used by the handmaids. When all of this had been decided, we got on to the builders and decorators. During the time that the house was being refurbished, the handmaids came to stay with me at Bridgemount. I had some modifications done to Bridgemount to increase sleeping capacity and I had the breakfast-room table moved into the study, so that the breakfast-room could be made into a small chapel. For that period, the archbishop assigned a chaplain to us, and we had the privilege of having Mass every morning, and the added privilege of having the Blessed Sacrament under the roof. In those days it was possible to get work done quickly and done well and in no time at all, St Joseph's was ready. We opened on 2 July 1957. Fr Concannon said Mass for us in the house and from then on a whole new era began.

Our aim, as I have already said, was to provide accommodation for invalids who, because of living a distance from the shrine, and being unable to afford any accommodation, were unable to come to Knock. In the beginning we contacted hospitals, county homes and other institutions where patients had been confined for years without any hope whatever of getting home – indeed the reality was that few had homes to go to. We could take very few at that time, but even so, it was soon very obvious that St Joseph's was becoming a runaway success. Requests to come to us were growing rapidly and it was always difficult to say no. It was small wonder: the house, though small in size, was big in welcomes. In it, we opened up a week of home comforts, care and affection for those poor people who for so long had nothing other than regimentation and the drab institutional life then available to them. Those were the bad old days and it is difficult to believe that such miserable conditions ever existed. However, before the days of even minimal social security payments, and particularly before a general awareness of the requirements of the permanently sick and disadvantaged was created, those conditions were indeed a grim reality.

The tiny garden, which was looked after by Margaret,

provided a hint of colour, a few fresh flowers, and plenty of little things such as herbs were grown, small things in themselves, but touches that made a world of difference to people so long denied even simple basic pleasures. The handmaids cooked the best of fresh natural food, and in the evening, the day's devotions done, the patients gathered round the turf fire to sing songs or just to chat and make friends. Each morning they had Mass in their own tiny chapel, a rare privilege for most of them, after lunch they were taken out to the shrine for devotions, and last thing at night they returned to the chapel for evening prayers before being tucked up comfortably in bed. It was a blissful week for almost all of them, and they left us with great sadness, often full of tears, and begging us to take them again in the coming year.

Understandably, we were soon inundated with requests to come to St Joseph's and our helpers at all points were being asked to take this one and that. Patients returning to hospitals in Dublin spread the word about us among others and soon it was impossible to make all who wanted to come understand that we just did not have the space. It was quite obvious that we would have to do something about expansion, but it seemed a difficult problem to solve. One day I saw an advertisement in a local newspaper for the sale of some pre-fab huts which appeared to have a large capacity. It seemed that when the new Regional Hospital was being built in Galway, the hospital administrators could find no space large enough to house the nursing staff who had to be uprooted and housed while awaiting their new quarters, so they erected a series of pre-fab units to accommodate them. Now, those huts having served their purpose were to be sold off by auction. I got the notion that perhaps one of them could solve a problem for us, for the moment at least, and so I went to Knock to talk about it with Fr Concannon.

Together we went through the pros and cons, and in the end, decided that we should pursue the idea, as it would tide us over for the time being at least. We then got in touch with John Cunnane, a local builder, who, over the years, had done a good deal of work for us, and he was someone I had always found helpful and dependable. He was of the opinion that the huts would be in good condition as the Galway building had been completed quickly, and they had not been lying around for years. In the end, I asked him if he would go to the auction and bid for one of them for us, which he did, and in due course he had it collected and brought to Knock. For a while there was great fuss as to where it might be located, which seemed extraordinary in view of the decision to buy it. There was a grass verge beside the presbytery which was big enough to take it, but that being church property, appeared to be out of bounds, as, according to the experts, there was some fine point about not being able to designate it for anything other than specific church use. In the end, the archbishop got around it somehow by a clear understanding that everything about the building would be, once again, 'temporary', as if given the fabric of the building, it could possibly be anything else. In due course it was erected and quickly equipped with beds, plus a few small comforts, but basically, it had only the bare essentials for simple living. The food had to be taken across fom the main kitchen and there was always the problem of trying to keep it hot. However, because of that little extra space, we were able to increase our quota of patients and we were always packed to capacity.

Patients spoke about the joy of being able to spend a week in a comfortable natural home, where their every need was anticipated and every problem understood. There were many comments too, on the peace and happiness experienced in the house and the wish expressed to return. Before long, some members of the St Vincent de Paul Society in Dublin who visited those patients on a regular basis, came to hear about this place, St Joseph's at Knock. As the subject came up again and again they wondered what sort of wonderful formula we possessed to inspire such glowing praise, so a few of them, in particular Mr Con Smith of Smith's Garages, then the main Irish agent for Renault cars, came to Knock with a group of his Vincent de Paul colleagues to see it for themselves. They saw us for what we were, and they, being businessmen, saw at once that our big problem was space.

Once again, Providence seemed to guide our venture, call it coincidence if you will, but the development from then on was extraordinary. As soon as Mr Smith and his colleagues got back to Dublin and had their first meeting, they decided to do something about St Joseph's. First they spoke to Fr Benedict, ODC, who visited the hospitals regularly and was a priest they knew very well. They asked him if he knew anything about Knock and particularly about St Joseph's and the conditions prevailing there. As it so happened, Fr Benedict was an old friend of ours, a friendship going back to the early days, so one could say he was an inspired choice. They told him that they would be prepared to finance an extension to St Joseph's, if we would be prepared to run it exactly as the existing house was being run with our own group of handmaids. Fr Benedict listened to all they had to say and he then suggested that they should write to me. Before long, I had a letter from Mr Smith outlining to me their offer which, in terms of a gift, was then very generous and substantial. I suppose one could say that it was the first meaningful charitable development at Knock. It was not the end of Mr Smith's personal generosity either, as he sent me a very worthwhile cheque for St Joseph's every year from then till the end of his life.

To digress for a moment, it is worth noting that since we first opened the doors of St Joseph's, we have never had to ask for anything. I remember one occasion when we were dealing with the pre-fab and were in dire need of financial help – we needed £500 badly, and did not have it. £500 may seem a small sum today, but in the 1950s it was quite a sum. At that point a pilgrim called to see us and, taking me aside, said that she felt we needed money for equipment, food and all the other things we had to buy and, opening her bag, she handed me a cheque for £500.

On receipt of Mr Smith's letter I sent it directly to the archbishop asking him to advise me on how I should reply, and he contacted me to say that he was looking into the possibilities. Before long, he phoned and asked me if I would meet him in Dublin on a day to be decided. For that meeting, he was planning to line up an architect, Mr Johnny Robinson, Fr Concannon and John Cunnane to discuss a completely new building. He told me that all three of them had together examined the existing St Joseph's thoroughly, and they were satisfied that nothing worthwhile could be done to improve the house, as the structure was unsuitable for extension on such a scale. A couple of days after that I travelled to Dublin and went to Wynn's Hotel in Lower Abbey Street to meet them as arranged.

I shall never forget my dismay on seeing the plans. The site for the new St Joseph's was right in the middle of the shrine grounds, or rather the grounds as they are today. In those days, the site was a little away from the shrine, cut off by a path, which was then a right of way to Byrne's pub. Some years later that right of way, and the pub itself were bought by Canon Horan, as he then was, and the path is now part of the Basilica forecourt. Acquisition of land was always very difficult, except in the very early days. Way back in the beginning we were convinced that the shrine would develop at some stage, and we spent many hours discussing it with Canon Grealy and asking him to buy. He did eventually buy the processional field immediately in front of the old church, together with one higher up the hill. However, there was still a long garden which divided the two fields, so that processions had to come out onto the main road to get from one field to the other, a very unsatisfactory arrangement for all concerned, even for the traffic passing through. This piece of land was held by one owner.

One day shortly after Liam's death, having visited his grave, I was walking back to my car when the owner of that piece of land came to sympathise with me. He was walking along an old path to his shed, which stood more or less where the clinic stands today. He expressed his sympathy adding that he hoped I would still be able to carry on working for Knock and acknowledged all we had already achieved. I replied that it was going to be very difficult for me to do so, and it would depend mainly on the co-operation I was likely to get. I told him that conditions were almost impossible without space for the estimated numbers of pilgrims. He assured me that he would be pleased to help in any way he could, and stressed that I must not hesitate to ask him. Very soon after that, we, the society, asked the archbishop to negotiate with him about the obtruding garden, which he did, and it was bought, thus giving clear access to the shrine from the hill, making a fine processional field.

Remembering all those difficulties, and all the land problems to which, over the years, I had become very sensitive, I was very uneasy about the whole layout. There were grave doubts in my mind about the wisdom of the plan, and I said so several times to the archbishop. I felt that the day might come when it would be necessary to build a new church, but he assured me that he had examined every inch of the grounds, and there never would be any plans for that particular area. However, I was not convinced, and I wanted it put on record that the choice of site was solely theirs which, after much discussion, and further efforts to allay my fears, was done. We then got on with talking about the plans in detail and they listened to my suggestions about the specific requirements of a 'rest house' as distinct from an institution for invalids.

The old house had served us well, and taught us many lessons as to the ideal corridor width for wheelchairs, heights for beds and their fittings, the vital finishings such as grab rails, bath aids, towel rails and the thousand other aids which are necessary. Most of those things are commonplace today with a more enlightened attitude towards the disabled, but in those days the provision of such essentials and their precise siting did not arise for most architects. I returned home next day on the train, and all along the way my thoughts were occupied with a list of things that would be required to furnish and equip the house. Looking at the figures we were working on then, and the prices when we got round to final quotations, it seems almost laughable. An important item such as a bed, fully dressed and well dressed at that, was listed at £55, today that figure would not buy a blanket or a decent pair of sheets. However, the costs were relative and realistic at the time, and somehow, through the generosity of pilgrims and hundreds of other generous people, we managed to equip it.

I still had the problem of staff to run the house. We had a few excellent people already, but we were about to double capacity, and a new purpose-built house would inevitably call for a variety of skills, in particular, nursing. Among handmaids at the time we had a young public health nurse, May Bailey, and I wondered to myself about asking her to join us in the new venture. May had a splendid nursing record. She had been a prize-winning student all the way and, having qualified, she had gone on to take several specialist courses. She had not long been appointed to her permanent and pensionable position in County Roscommon and the thought of asking her to give it up, as that was the reality, seemed almost ludicrous. However, I had already singled her out as a deeply religious girl and anyhow, there was no harm in asking. On her next day on duty in Knock I took her aside and told her all I could have told her about St Joseph's and our concern about getting suitable staff. I was also very careful to point out that such a commitment from her, or indeed from anybody, would be, of necessity, entirely voluntary, and there could be no question of payment of any kind. To my complete amazement, May offered without any hesitation to become a completely dedicated handmaid, a very special section of the handmaids, and to resign from her job. I went to great pains then to emphasise the risk she was about to take, and the uncertainty about the future of St Joseph's, as nobody then knew how it might turn out.

I have never known anybody with such complete trust in God as May had. For her, there was no doubt whatever; the work at St Joseph's was for God and for Our Lady and as such, would have to flourish. In the face of such rock solid faith there was little room for reason. She went home that night, and next day gave her notice to the council. Very soon after that she got in touch with me to say that she was ready to come. On the day she was coming to us, she drove herself to the station where she was to catch the train. Then, as she felt she would not need her new car at Knock, she gave the keys to her brother who was seeing her off, and with complete confidence in God, she set out for St Joseph's. By any standards, it was a supreme sacrifice, but in the light of all that was to happen in the years that were to follow, it was only a beginning. May ran Sr Joseph's with calm effeciency, caring for the hundreds of men and women who passed through its doors. This she did with kindness beyond measure, and a deep concern for their welfare. In all those years, May was on duty every season twenty-four hours every day, often being called several times during the night to help somebody who was ill. The sick loved her, as indeed they should, since she was a true friend to all of them, constantly aware of their needs, with never a thought of self.

About the same time, another young handmaid, Agnes White, decided that she would come. Everybody who came to St Joseph's knew and loved Agnes, a gracious girl who, like May, also gave up a well paid and secure position. She too spent her years with the sick, overseeing their meals, noting their likes and dislikes, but always ready with a smile and a helping hand no matter how tired she might have been feeling herself. It is heartening to note that there were people to make such a commitment. They are rare, but thank God, they still exist. Latterly, Mary Neary, another splendid handmaid, joined the ranks, and in no time at all she had acquired all the necessary skills, and was able to take over the complete running of St Joseph's, when conditions called on her to do so, and this she did with complete confidence and excellence for several years.

In this, of course, she had the support of a number of trained nurses who came as often as they could, as well as the generous help from several handmaids and other voluntary workers.

The foundation stone for the new St Joseph's was laid on 22 August 1968 and it opened its doors very soon after. In his address that day, our archbishop, Dr Cunnane said, 'Let our prayers be that this building may stand as a monument to the untiring zeal of so many apostolic workers for the sick.' There is no doubt about the fact that this apostolic zeal was a notable feature of the work that was carried out at St Joseph's from the opening of the first house in

1957 until the end of the century and beyond, over forty years later.

In later years however, social conditions were changing and full employment, coupled with a new prosperity, changed the course of events. Public Health and support services were changing rapidly and patients had access to a fair degree of health care. The dire poverty that prevailed in our early years had, thank God, become a thing of the past. Above all else, however, there was an acute shortage of nurses, which made the running of a fully staffed voluntary home almost impossible. The climax came for us with the Foot and Mouth epidemic which caused all functions and fixtures to be cancelled. It was indeed a sad summer for me, and for all of us, to see the doors of our cherished St Joseph's closed, but we were absolutely helpless in this matter. However, Providence has once again intervened and the Brothers of St John of God, highly respected carers that they are, have taken on St Joseph's and will, please God, run it as a hostel for the sick who wish to come to stay for a few days and pray; however, we must wait and see exactly how they will be able to organise it. The main body of invalids and the sick still come on pilgrimage on Sundays, weekdays and, in particular, on the Last Thursday of each month when there are special devotions for them. They are, as always, looked after by the handmaids and stewards, and in these days of full and plenty, this is in itself a singular blessing.

The Dedicated Handmaids, which are a special section of the main body of handmaids, form a group called the 'Pious Union'. They take vows as religious do, and give a lot of their time to prayer. They can be extern members, following their own professions, or work, or intern when they live in St Brigid's, a house built for them by Monsignor Horan, and given over to us after the Holy Father's visit.

This is a house of formation, of prayer, a base for retreat and general meditation. It is the very core of the handmaids' calling, with the motto, 'You did it to me' and in its dedicated and prayerful way of life it may yet provide the answer to many of the problems of today.

13

The story of the statues

F rom the first moment that Liam and I began to take an interest in Knock, we knew that it was essential to have some sort of fitting representation of the Apparition placed at the gable, so that pilgrims could appreciate its full magnitude. During those early years we became more and more convinced that very few people appreciated the wonder of the vision that had been seen, or understood its possible significance. As soon as the Knock Shrine Society was founded in 1935, one of the principal items on the agenda for our first meeting was the enhancement of the gable. This was discussed in great detail and was one of our main concerns at the time. The altar that was erected there in 1940 was intended merely as a shelter for the celebrants at the ceremonies and was accepted by all of us purely as a temporary arrangement. All the time we were conscious of the fact that a permanent shrine would have to be considered at some future date but, at the beginning, considerable ground work had to be completed before any comprehensive plans could be formulated. It was an important development which could not be undertaken in haste or in isolation; the whole future of the shrine was still uncertain and we, the society, then the only people who were prepared to take responsibility for this, had to make haste slowly.

It would be incorrect to conclude however, that the matter was set aside or was forgotten. During those formative years, we discussed plans for a shrine with various people who were acknowledged to be authorities on such matters, and we came to the conclusion that to be acceptable

His holiness, Pope John Paul II at Knock Shrine
– 'the goal of my journey to Ireland'

The beautiful white marble statuary representing the Knock Apparition. It
was blessed by Pope John Paul II when he visited Knock Shrine,
30 September 1979

The Basilica packed to capacity, with bishops and priests surrounding the altar, 15 August 1979

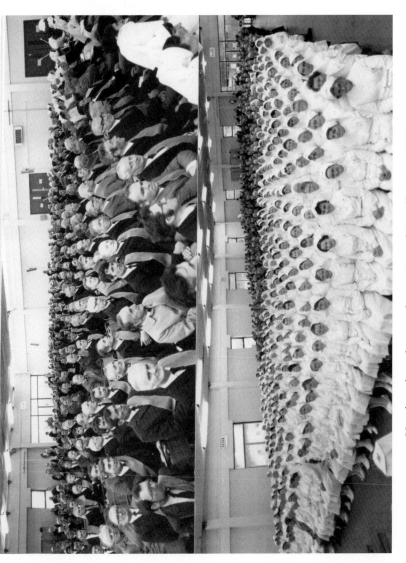

Handmaids and stewards at a Day of Recollection, 1984

The Shrine today, surrounded by flowers

The Chapel of Reconciliation built by Monsignor Dominick Grealy,
opened 15 July 1990

St Joseph's Rest House, which replaced the old one,
run by the dedicated handmaids for 43 years

The Basilica in summer sunshine

Dame Judy Coyne after the papal visit in 1979

Golden Jubilee of Knock Shrine Society, 1985. L–R: Msgr J. Horan, His Excellency Dr G. Alibrandi, Papal Nuncio, Dame Judy Coyne, Archbishop J. Cunnane

1997: Archbishop Michael Neary conferring the honour of Dame Commander of the Order of St Sylvester on Dame Judy Coyne

President Mary McAleese with a group of handmaids at a novena in Knock in 1998. Front row: Msgr D. Grealy, Dame Judy Coyne, President Mary McAleese; back row: Mrs N. Forde, Mrs P. Riordain, Miss N. Neary, Mrs P. Higgins

to the Irish people or indeed to anybody else, an accurate and beautiful representation of the Apparition would have to be put in place. From time to time, while the last surviving witness, Mrs O'Connell still lived, we commissioned various artists to prepare pictures following the descriptions we gave them, and in fairness to them they did the best they could. However, when we took those pictures to her, a woman who was scrupulously correct in every detail of her accounts, she was at pains to tell us that despite their fine efforts, nobody could make pictures to look like the Apparition, as the figures had been, as she said, 'made of light'. However, we felt that given the right artist, somebody with sensitivity, genuine artistry and above all, inspiration, a worthy representation could be achieved. Time and again, we spoke to the archbishop about a permanent shrine, but on each occasion we were told that the time was not yet right.

Twenty-five years after founding the society, and to mark our Silver Jubilee in 1960, I approached him yet again, asking if we could erect the shrine. By that time, I suppose he had got tired of my asking or perhaps he genuinely thought that the time to do something about it had indeed come. We had in the few years which had gone before, progressed significantly, the shrine had been spoken of on Vatican Radio by Fr Conway, we had had our banner honoured in Rome and we'd had the processional statue crowned, so it seemed a logical progression. At long last, he gave us permission to go ahead and we were ready for the moment. It was agreed that an open international competition would be held which would invite sculptors to submit models of statues, along our given guidelines, of all the reported figures, and we would offer prizes, finally commissioning the best work. This was done, and in the end, the work of a well-known Roman sculptor, Professor Lorenzo Ferri was selected and he was commissioned by the archbishop to carry it out. Professor Ferri was a remarkable man who had a very fine reputation as a sculptor. Among other things, he had, for thirty-eight years given his spare time to working on the Holy Shroud of Turin in order to reconstruct an image of Christ's body as it hung on the cross and later lay in the tomb. From the experience gained through that work, he had carved a splendid figure of Christ in white marble, and from that, he then carved a head of Our Lady also in marble, having copied her features from the statue of her Divine Son, reasoning that as Christ had only one human parent, his mother, his features should resemble hers. All of this was very relevant to the work as we saw it.

It was agreed that Professor Ferri would submit three sets of clay models of all the proposed statues in different sizes before he began to work on the final carving. He was completely enamoured of the account of the Apparition; being a devout man, the emphasis on the Mass appealed to him. From the beginning he was almost as concerned as we were that the work would be correct in every detail. It was decided that on receipt of the first set of models the members of our council would indicate any changes required and these would be then incorporated in the second. It was also agreed that when these final changes, if any, had been carried out, Professor Ferri would come to Knock, bringing the modified models with him, so that we could get a clear idea of how the finished figures might look. It was a big undertaking, and there was no doubt in our minds about the quality of the work we expected. After some little time, Professor Ferri did come, to sense the atmosphere for himself, to study the surroundings and to take detailed measurements of the gable. He stayed on for several days absorbing the ambience and thinking deeply about the proposed work. When, many years afterwards, we saw the completed statues it was quite obvious that he had captured every aspect perfectly, but all of that was then a very long way off.

As soon as the final set of models was ready for inspection, the archbishop phoned one day and asked me if I would go to Rome to make sure that all the details were correct before he gave the final instruction to complete the work. I hesitated as I fully realised the responsibility I was being asked to take on and I knew that if anything were to go wrong, then I alone would be to blame. I said as much to the archbishop, but he brushed my doubts aside and made it quite clear that he wished me to go. I suppose it was inevitable, since from the very beginning Liam and I had been so involved with getting this particular aspect of the shrine to materialise. He was also aware that during the gathering of material for the first book, I had spoken to Mrs O'Connell on numerous occasions, and he also knew that I had checked and re-checked all the descriptive details and was fully conversant with them.

Mrs O'Connell was always delighted to hear about our work to further the promotion of Knock and was most willing to help in any way she could. She had a wonderful memory and one day when I was talking to her she told me that she could close her eyes and see the vision all over again. I remember her distinctly that day as she stood by the sideboard in her room in order to show me exactly how Our Lady had stood. She emphasised particularly the way she had held her hands, holding her own in the same position; the angle of her head, and as she said, 'her lovely upturned eyes'. She had spoken frequently of the heavenly expression on Our Lady's countenance and of the light that seemed to come out from her figure, much brighter than the light that came from St Joseph or St John, but not as bright as the light from the Lamb.

She described in detail Our Lady's robe which fell ungirdled and in full folds from the throat, with what she called 'something like ruching down the front'. She spoke of St John as a young handsome man wearing garments and a mitre of a type she had never seen before, but which she described in great detail and which were later identified as eastern vestments. When I asked her whether she thought St John had been reading or preaching, she said without any hesitation, 'preaching'. Even though no words had been spoken at Knock, her own impression was that St John had been preaching about the Lamb. She demonstrated the position in which he had stood, the altar and Lamb on his left, with Our Lady on his right, and she was most particular about that point. She was also very definite about the fact that St Joseph had stood with his head only, not his whole body, bowed. That particular point was unusual, as most traditional representations of St Joseph depicted him noticeably stooped, and Mrs O'Connell was at pains to point out this difference. All of this and a great deal more gave me a unique opportunity to get first-hand information, information which as given by her was definite and lucid, and was in itself enough to leave me with a very clear picture in my mind of a truly magnificent manifestation.

As I had been to Rome for the Knock shrine Marian pilgrimage just a few years before, I had no particular desire to make the journey so soon again. Above all, I did not welcome the responsibility, but in the light of the archbishop's reasoning, it seemed irresponsible to refuse to go. So after some further discussion, and putting my full confidence in Our Lady's direction, I did as requested and made plans to go to Rome once again. By that time, the pilgrimage season at Knock had ended for that particular year, and there was a little time to sit down and make plans for the trip.

From the moment the work on the statues was commissioned, the archbishop had requested Fr Conway to supervise their actual making and this he had very generously consented to do. I have already described Fr Conway's great kindness to us when we went to Rome on our Marian Year pilgrimage; by 1960 he had been elevated to a 'monsignor', and was still attached to the Irish College. Since he spoke Italian fluently, and knew the city and the people who mattered thorougly, he was ideally suited to take decisions on our behalf and resolve any difficult problems that might have arisen. More important by far however, was the fact that he took a deep interest in the entire project and, as it turned out, he never spared himself in ensuring that everything would be done perfectly. At an early stage in the proceedings, he had translated the depositions of the fifteen witnesses for Professor Ferri into Italian, and made himself available to him for consultation all the way through. At the same time, he was in direct touch with us about the progress of the work, so we were kept very well briefed.

When I had made all arrangements for the journey and had asked Our Lady again and again for her help in the task I was about to take on, I flew to Rome. It was 4 November 1960. I don't remember a great deal about the flight, there wasn't anything very special to get excited about, it was going to be a short stay, a couple of days, just a visit to the sculptor's studio to make sure that everything was all right. I could then ask him to go ahead and finish the statues and it would be possible to return home without undue delay. That, at least, was my plan. I could not have known as I stepped on to an Aer Lingus flight at Dublin airport that November morning, that my 'couple of days' was about to extend to a very long stay in Rome, and at the same time, become a time of great anxiety for all concerned.

I had arranged to stay again at the Hotel Columbus. I had stayed there before and as I had found it satisfactory then, there seemed to be no reason to change. It was convenient for morning Mass, and I already knew it, which was a very important consideration when travelling alone. When I arrived at Ciampino airport I was met by Pino Cuccari, who was manager of Professor Ferri's studio. Pino had spent several years in America so he spoke English very well, and he had stayed at Bridgemount when he had come with the sculptor to Ireland some little time before, so he was no stranger to me or to the business in hand. He came to the airport to greet me carrying a huge bouquet of flowers, a gracious gesture which I soon learned was typically Italian; there were flowers on so many occasions, any excuse would do for giving them, so one soon got used to that charming custom.

Next morning after Mass, Pino came to collect me at the hotel and take me to the professor's studio. It was quite a distance from the hotel, on the Via Felice Cavalotti, a very interesting quarter of the city, quite near to the Gianicola, with its famous views over Rome, but on that occasion, sightseeing was not on my agenda. He had a studio that had been adapted specially for the work as it required a large amount of space to accommodate it. On arrival, I was delighted to find that the models were excellent in all details, except for two things, and I suppose with hindsight, these two things were among the most important aspects of the Apparition. I was not satisfied with the expression on Our Lady's face, despite the fact that her features, which had been copied from the statue which followed the studies on the shroud, were beautiful, he had not quite captured the portrayal of enrapt ecstatic contemplation as I had hoped.

Also the Lamb, as I saw it in any case, seemed to me to be too Italianate, thin, with a very long neck, maybe even Biblical, but not at all like those soft fluffy lambs familiar to us in Ireland which the witnesses would have recognised, and which I felt we should have. The sculptor was at a loss to know what I meant, as I'm quite sure he had never seen an Irish lamb, but he did his best to please me and adjusted the model as I suggested. After a great deal of chopping and changing he finally announced that he would have to get a live lamb and have another go at it, so he asked me if I would go with Pino to the hills outside Rome to select the type of lamb I had in mind from a flock of sheep which he knew we would find there. I was only too glad to do anything that might help, but I expressed doubt about getting a young lamb at that time of the year. I was assured however, that that would present no problem, and so when the necessary arrangements and enquiries had been completed, we set off one morning in a mini, of all things, driving at top speed to the mountains.

It was a journey of about sixty miles and we had taken the sculptor's young son, Leonardo, to look after the lamb on the journey back. Thinking about it now the idea of taking a live lamb in a mini, or indeed in any car, all the way from the mountains back to the middle of the city of Rome seems to have been far fetched, and yet at the time we did not give it a second thought. It was something that had to be done, so we got on with doing it. As my plan had been to go to Rome for just a 'couple of days', I had taken with me only a small case, and enough clothes for such a short stay. My court shoes, suede ones at that, and the only type of shoes I had with me, were hardly suitable for flocking sheep on a mountainside. However, we were most fortunate in finding just one lamb in the whole flock which looked like the lambs I had been used to seeing. He was just three weeks old, and we paid in lira the equivalent of thirty shillings to the old country woman who was selling him. She was like any country woman one might encounter at home in the west in those days, dressed entirely in black, and she seemed very satisfied with her price.

During the journey back to Rome, young Leonardo, who was thrilled to have got custody of the lamb, took off his jacket and wrapped it round him, no doubt a particular type of loving care not especially appreciated by its recipient, but the journey back was quite without incident. When we got to the studio however, it was a different story; there was great excitement as the little creature was still so young that it had to be hand fed. Before this was done, however, the staff insisted on leading him to a nearby park to see if they could tempt him to nibble grass, and for the outing, he was tethered by a pink satin ribbon. When the excitement died down a bit, we fed him from a baby's bottle, which somebody had acquired, not from a chemist as one might expect, but from a nearby trattoria – nothing like keeping it all in the family! In no time at all, the lamb became the pampered pet of the studio, scampering in and out through the statues. While the sculptor made the new model, the lamb stood on a table and, as requested, I held him. This time the model was a great success.

Also claiming the affections of the staff was the inevitable studio cat, a fat cat who had all rights reserved on the one and only chair. He sat on it purring loudly until I came to take it, then as soon as I had sat down, he hopped on to my lap, and every time I stood up to look at something which was being shown to me, he hopped back on the chair again. When the professor occasionally gave me books of illustrations for consultation, or something else he wanted me to examine, I used the cat as a book prop. I had no choice, he was not getting down and he seemed to rather like the attention. All things considered, it was a very natural and happy studio, and they certainly did everything possible to try to make my long hours there pleasant and comfortable.

Several years later, I heard quite by accident from Canon Michael Moran, who was then parish priest of Newport,

Co. Mayo, that when the lamb had grown too big for the studio, he was given to the community of the Little Company of Mary in Rome. There was some talk apparently of having presented him to the Holy Father at the celebrations for St Agnes's Feast, when once again he was decked out in satin bows. In the end, the sisters took him to their convent high in the hills at beautiful Fiesole above Florence. There he had the freedom of the wide open space of their delightful garden, and he became a cherished pet, encouraged to make frequent trips to the kitchen where he was given all sorts of tasty tit bits. From other reports of him since received, he lived out his happy life being totally spoiled until he died, and he was buried somewhere within the garden boundaries.

Meantime, the days went by and I sat in the sculptor's studio while he tried again and again to capture the desired expression on Our Lady's face, especially in the eyes. He worked feverishly to a background of classical music, mostly Beethoven, but he played other composers as well which was very pleasant for all of us. It was an anxious time for all concerned however, and although the tension was not particularly apparent, it was there nonetheless. Now and then when I think about it today, I marvel at the patience, courtesy and humility of that great sculptor, in the face of my demands. It was small wonder that one day, after several unsuccessful alterations to the model, he exclaimed almost in despair, 'Madame wants the divine, I can only give her the human'. This frustrating experimenting went on for almost two weeks, and at the time it seemed as if it never would come right.

Each evening on his way home from his work in the Vatican, Monsignor Conway would call to the studio, chat to the sculptor and to me, and enquire generally as to how things were going. There were times when I could see no progress at all, and he sensed this. On those occasions, monsignor would say to me that I must bear with it and see it out, and I must not in any circumstances consider going home until I was completely satisfied. I am quite sure that were it not for his constant encouragement, I would have abandoned it and gone. Once or twice I wondered if I would ever be satisfied, but such doubts were fleeting and I found courage in prayer. In such circumstances, however, I suppose it was inevitable, that Professor Ferri, who suffered from a heart condition, might have problems, and not surprisingly, in due course he succumbed to an attack and was ordered by his doctor to rest in bed. He was very reluctant to obey, since there was so much still unresolved and I was there in Rome waiting. Monsignor Conway, probably fearing that I might abandon the whole thing, acted with his customary good sense and diplomacy and suggested that I should leave Rome for a few days until the situation improved. He decided that a short spell away from the scene would do me no harm either, since by that time I was becoming very concerned about the whole undertaking and the tension was becoming apparent. I was very conscious of my responsibility and the lack of progress after such a long time. Some of that anxiety must have by then become obvious and that did not help matters.

A family relative, Sr Perpetua Hayes, who was Mother Superior of a very large hospital in Naples, which was run by her order, the Medical Missionaries, had invited me when I first arrived in Rome to spend a few days with her, as she thought that it would be nice for me to visit Naples. In normal circumstances, nothing would have been more delightful, but at the time, I had declined, as I expected to be going home in a couple of days and, as always, there was a lot of work to be done. Providence had quickly changed that, and I now gladly accepted her invitation and phoned her to tell her about the change of plans. I travelled to Naples on the train, and on arrival I was made very welcome by the sisters at their huge Clinica Mediterranea on the Via Orazio. At once, they made me feel at home, they had beautiful home-cooked food for me, which was heaven after the hotel food, good though it had been, but above all, responsible medical staff that they were, they recognised immediately the signs of exhaustion. On the evening I arrived they sent me to bed soon after dinner and I slept soundly all night. In the morning, I discovered that they had taken away all my laundry while I slept, it must have been indeed a deep sleep, and left it back to me, dry, fresh and fragrant, before I woke. Anybody who has been completely jaded and travel weary will understand the feeling of comfort and refreshment that a long deep sleep, even without such caring attention, can bring.

Next day, fully restored, they took me by car along the entire length of the magnificent Amalfi coast, and on that magical trip the blue Mediterranean slept calmly in sunshine in the arc of its famous bay. We called at Pompeii and saw some of the wonders of that ancient place, but in particular its impressive Basilica with its own very famous Madonna. For a little time among all that warmth and undreamed of beauty, it was almost possible to forget about worries. Sr Perpetua had not told me at that stage of the greatest treat which she had arranged and was still keeping as a surprise for me, a visit to San Giovanni to assist at Padre Pio's Mass. When, later that evening she told me about this, I was thrilled beyond measure and next morning, with one of her sisters, Sr Maria Anne Travers, I set out by train as she had planned. As we began the long journey across Italy I felt certain that our prayers, which on that morning were for the successful completion of the statues, would be answered. Sure of the outcome and relaxed from the rest and the sunshine, I settled back in my seat just to gaze through the train windows and enjoy the scenery. I remember marvelling at the russet fields that seemed to fly towards and past our windows as the train sped through the countryside. When eventually it slowed down at some country halt, Sr Maria Anne showed me the reason for the rosy glow, for those unusual looking fields were packed with row upon row of ripe red apples which were being harvested.

Very early next morning, Friday 18 November, we were present at Padre Pio's memorable Mass and it was an experience of a lifetime. We prayed as fervently as we could that Professor Ferri would soon recover and be inspired to complete the models as true to the description of the Apparition as was humanly possible. As the Mass finished I felt a great peace and a strange awareness that somehow Padre Pio knew of our intention. We returned to Naples that evening very happy indeed with our experience.

Next day, Monsignor Conway phoned us from Rome, to say that Professor Ferri was feeling well again, almost as if Our Lady had arranged for me to take special leave and had given me time to make that journey, so as soon as I got the message, I decided to return without delay.

Next day, Sunday, I took the train back to Rome and early on Monday morning, on reaching the studio, I was astounded to find three large new models outside the door. When I left Rome Professor Ferri had been seriously ill, and it seemed extraordinary that he could have completed so much work in the short time since I'd heard that he was feeling better. One glance at the face of Our Lady was sufficient to convince me that an entirely new likeness had been created. I could hardly believe what I was seeing, and with boundless joy I exclaimed that it was absolutely perfect. When Professor Ferri realised that I was so delighted, and particularly when I told him that the expression was as I had visualised all along, it was his turn to be amazed and he then told me a most extraordinary story.

Very early on the previous Friday morning, 18 November, he was lying in bed feeling very unwell, when suddenly he felt some spiritual force which positively took over and compelled him. He jumped out of bed and, taking time to put on only his pants and his shoes, he ran downstairs locking all the doors securely so that nobody could disturb him, not even his staff who would be arriving for work in a few hours. Then with feverish haste he began to re-make the models. Entirely unaided, he completed the task in three hours without stopping, something that would normally have taken the same number of weeks. In all his life he had never experienced anything like the driving force and the energy which had motivated him. He had no idea that I had been to San Giovanni Rotondo and he was astonished when I told him of my special request during Mass. When he heard the time that Mass had been celebrated, he realised at once that it was at that same hour he had felt the strange force which drove him to complete the work. We were both entirely convinced that the favour was granted through Padre Pio's Mass. I was told at the time that Professor Ferri assisted at 6 a.m. Mass every day while he worked on the Knock statues. He felt greatly privileged to be representing such a wonderful Eucharistic Apparition, and he wanted it to be the greatest work of his life. He looked forward to the day when he could admire his splendid statuary fittingly enshrined at Knock, but I am sorry to say he did not live to see it.

As soon as I possibly could, I made arrangements to get home as I had been in Rome for far too long and I was almost afraid to imagine the mountain of letters that would be awaiting me. It was not possible to get a direct flight at such short notice, so I got a British Airways flight to London, and changed there to an Aer Lingus flight to get me home.

But the story of the statues was not finished then. There was still a good deal of trouble ahead for Monsignor Conway, all the time until the agreed completion date, and when that was all done, the unforeseen problem of enormously heavy insurance costs for their journey to Ireland. With his usual calm, he organised all of that and took delivery of them at Carrara officially for us. They were shipped to Ireland on a boat called *The Iona* and arrived in Dublin Bay on 15 August 1963. As it so happened, there was a dock strike when they arrived and they had to wait for several weeks before there was any question of their being unloaded. When eventually this happened, they were dumped at the docks during the last troubled days of the strike. Then there were endless problems about getting them to Knock, as they were exceptionally heavy, so a very heavy lorry had to be obtained to transport them. John Cunnane, reliable as ever, came to our assistance and, though it certainly was a 'long load' in the full sense of the word, he got them safely home. If one were looking for coincidences on that occasion, they arrived on the eve of 8 September.

The shrine, as designed by Professor Ferri was meant to be placed well above the heads of the people, with the figures, which are considerably larger than life size, standing in front of and within representational mosaics. Side panels which incorporated imagined likenesses of the witnesses as they had stood on that rain swept Mayo landscape completed the story of the event. Behind the lamb, there were rising rays in gold and red-gold mosaic so that the figure would stand out, and all were to rest underneath a high domed roof. As it turned out, at the time the statues were delivered it was not opportune to erect the shrine, so they remained in their boxes. For sixteen years they were left there, lying in a hayshed beside Canon Horan's house.

Suddenly, in 1979, it was becoming clear that the Pope was about to accept the invitation to visit Knock for its centenary. Immediately before the official announcement of his visit was made, Canon Horan, anxious to get the shrine as well as the new church into good shape, remembered the statues. He phoned and told me then that he was about to get on with this and that he was planning to erect them. I held my breath and could not really believe what I was hearing. What would they find when they opened the boxes? After so many years the marble would probably be green and mildewed. To everybody's amazement, and in particular to mine, the opened boxes revealed the marble gleaming white. It was almost beyond belief, but as in all things connected with the shrine, I had long since given up being surprised by anything. Time was then very short, there was hardly enough of it to build the most basic shrine, which was made mostly of glass, none at all to think about a domed roof, or the intricacies of mosaic panels, which would have taken quite some time to put in place. However, we had a shrine for that day, and that was very important.

Early in the spring of 1991 however, the fabric of that shrine began to deteriorate, and several of the large glass panels crashed without warning. When the structure was examined it was declared to be unsafe and Monsignor Dominick Grealy, the parish priest, had no option but to rebuild it. For me, it was, once again, the intervention of Providence. Grateful as I had been for Canon Horan's brave efforts in erecting the shrine in time for the papal visit, I had always considered it to be makeshift and hurried. At last, after a lifetime, the time had come for a fitting shrine.

With extraordinary foresight, Monsignor Grealy commissioned Mr Andrzej Wejchert to design and build the new shrine. All through the winter and spring we watched as the huge cranes once again moved into place and lifted the precious statues away for safe keeping. Gradually, we saw form and grace rise from the rubble as a new chapel took shape and bit by bit become a fitting setting for the unique tableau. In limestone and local materials, with dark oak pews and capable of seating 150 pilgrims comfortably, though frequently it can be twice this number, it is a wonderful oasis of silence and prayer. Immediately prior to its completion, Monsignor Grealy phoned me one day and asked if I would come to Knock to be present for the final placing of the statues and advise on correct positioning. He too, was well aware of my close and detailed questioning of Mrs O'Connell on all aspects of the Apparition all those years ago. I went to Knock, my heart full of gratitude that I was at last seeing the realisation of the dream of my lifetime.

The complete tableau of beautifully wrought statuary which has now been placed precisely as described by the witnesses, was carved from snow white Carrara Marble, chosen because all the figures in the Apparition were clothed in white. It is of special interest that the figure of Our Lady and also that of the lamb, were made from the last block of the original Michelangelo marble in existence. Professor Ferri secured it because of its extraordinary quality of whiteness. It is also of particular interest and a thrilling end to that chapter of a singular story, that Pope John Paul personally blessed the statues when he came on 30 September 1979, to Knock which was, as he himself pointed out, 'the goal of my journey to Ireland'.

In this context, I feel it should be placed on record that Mrs Rose Virginia Jackman of California, paid for the statue of St John, in memory of Mrs M. A. Conway and she also paid for the altar, lamb and angels in memory of Monsignor Concannon who was parish priest at Knock for several years. The statue of Our Lady was paid for by the Knock shrine handmaids and stewards in memory of their first president, Liam Ua Cadhain.

14

Monsignor Horan
Centenary, Pope's visit and development at last

A ll through the years that I have worked at Knock I have stressed again and again, and I shall continue to do so for the rest of my life, my continuing amazement at the undeniable evidence of Providential direction in every-thing connected with it. Now towards the end of this long story I realise even more fully, how extraordinary that dir-ection has been. Over and over again, plans which at the time seemed to be getting nowhere, developed in the end even more perfectly than we had ever dreamed possible. I suppose our confidence during the years must now and then have been somewhat eroded. We had been working on the 'Cause' officially since 1935, in fact we had been aware of it and talking about it with serious concern since sometime in the early 1930s. It had been a long time even by the mid-1960s, and even then I could still see little pro-gress. As things have now turned out and recalling the rapid developments in latter years, I realise how perfectly everything had been designed, and marvel at the extraordi-nary precision with which every single facet of Knock's final triumph fitted together.

As I have already said, the new statues were delivered to Knock on the eve of 8 September 1963. On 9 September, a new curate came to Knock. He was Father James Horan. His appointment was not something we noticed as parti-cularly significant. Priests came and went and between one thing and another, made little difference to our work, as it was the parish priest who took decisions. I can recall little about Fr Horan in those early years, our paths were along separate lines, and his time was still in the future. Our main concern then was erecting the shrine, and on this we could make no progress whatever. After the first enthusiastic commissioning of the statues and the unusual experience I had had during their making, this was very hard for me to accept and I spent many anguished hours trying to work out what could be done. With hindsight however, though none of us realised it at the time, the delay was a singular blessing. Had we been able to go ahead then, I am quite sure that the shrine would have been inadequate: there was not much money to spend on it and who can tell what other set-backs might have spoiled it, or in some way clouded its significance.

We were then at the stage of the Second Vatican Council when Marian devotion, and everything pertaining to it, was being examined. Some theologians wanted change, or at least modifications and, always quick to spot any hint of dissent in such matters, this questioning was magnified by the media. For a time it was difficult to foretell what might be the outcome, but it gradually resolved itself in a very positive way. On 21 November 1964, Pope Paul VI, having concluded the third session of the council, invited twenty-four bishops who were custodians of Marian shrines around the world, to concelebrate Mass with him in St Peter's. Among the concelebrants that day was our own archbishop, Dr Cunnane, custodian of Knock shrine, another pointer, if one so chooses to analyse it, to 'coincidence'. Alongside the Marian devotion the general question of statues was also under debate. In churches all over the country they were being taken away completely and our own diocese was no exception. All of this was happening at a time when we were hoping to build the new shrine with full emphasis on the splendour of the Apparition: Mary, St Joseph and St John, with its centrepiece the Lamb of God, portrayed in

statues. It was inevitable that we would meet with difficulties. This no-go attitude lasted for quite a few years. I pre-
sume there was general indecision among the authorities
on such things, but it did not make it any easier for us, the
laity. Meantime we got on with the work in hand and prayed that everything would turn out for the best, which was
about all we could have done.

One cold January morning in 1964 I came in from Mass
and, having examined the mail and decided on the things
that had to be dealt with urgently, I scanned the paper
quickly, which is something I always do. I was fascinated by
a news account which I read, telling of a visit by Pope Paul
to the Holy Land and of how he had presented a Golden
Rose to the 'Bambino' at Bethlehem, there described as the
principal Marian shrine in the world. I read it through
several times, it was like a breath of fresh air, and a sign of
changing times. Here was the Pope, visiting a Marian shrine,
and presenting it with what was, apparently, the highest
token of honour that a Pope could bestow. At once an idea
crossed my mind, and nothing I could do would rid me of
it. If the Pope could visit one Marian shrine, I reasoned,
what was to stop him visiting another? The image of a
travelling Pope was then something new and at the back of
my mind I began to form the idea that one day, we might
get him to come to Knock. By that time I was beginning to
think of the centenary, and of the plans that should be
made to celebrate it. It was still fifteen years away, but for
an event of such a scale, plenty of time was needed. I was
very conscious of the lack of facilities at Knock, there was
not even an adequate church, not to mention a fitting
shrine. It seemed a bleak prospect. I had not reckoned however, on the extraordinary intervention of Providence. That
year, I was determined that if possible, the *Annual* would
carry an article on the Golden Rose and its history, as well

as an account of that unique papal visit and I asked Monsignor Dominic Conway if he would write it for us, which he very kindly did without any hesitation. I had known something about the Golden Rose from the time of our Marian Year pilgrimage to Rome ten years before, as it had been then mentioned as part of the story of the 'Salus Populi' picture which had itself been presented with the Golden Rose centuries before. However, I don't think it was something I had thought of in connection with Knock at that stage. Meantime, we proceeded with our usual work, season followed season, and for four years nothing, apparently, was being achieved.

I suppose the story of modern Knock began with the building of St Joseph's. The reason for its foundation and of the plans that were finalised while Fr Concannon was administrator (ADM) at Knock I have already given. Then on 22 August 1968, Dr Walsh came to bless the foundation stone for the new building. By that time Fr Concannon had been made parish priest elsewhere in the diocese and Fr Horan had taken his place as ADM at Knock. He had had a few years to survey the situation and had acquired in that time a sound knowledge of the requirements and the work of the shrine, and from the beginning he seemed to forge ahead from one major development to another. His achievements have already been well documented, indeed for several years he lived in the glare of publicity, sometimes welcome, sometimes not, but for us, the society, although we did not know it then, he was the catalyst we had been waiting for. It would not be true to say however, that his relationship with me or with the society was all easygoing, far from it. We had many tempestuous disagreements and many a meeting ended in disarray. However, it must be said that no matter how bitter the argument, he was man enough never to hold a grudge or grievance and it was all forgotten next time one met him. He realised that we were all working to promote the shrine and if a suggestion seemed to be a good one, he then considered it, and we worked it through. He was a man of immense vision who, when the initial short period of familiarisation with his new appointment was over, was quick to see all that needed to be done and more, and was not afraid to get on with it. He settled down quickly to working with us, and we were soon to recognise his methods and his merits, and in some strange way, realise that, through him, something significant was about to be achieved.

For several years leading up to the centenary, I had mentioned its importance in the editorial of each *Annual*. I must have become quite tiresome to all concerned as I began a countdown. Eleven years to go ... ten ... nine ... eight, etc., as year followed year and nothing special seemed to be happening. I was wrong of course, a great deal was happening, Fr Horan was pushing to get on with building the new church. At that time the church was spoken of purely as a shelter for pilgrims in bad weather, but as time progressed and architects became involved, the shelter acquired a more solid dimension. I was still most concerned about the shrine, but it was obvious that it was not then high on the list. Meantime, the building of St Joseph's went ahead and Fr Horan was to prove himself the hero of the hour when he succeeded in buying up rights-of-way and land adjoining the shrine. This was something that had eluded everybody else down the years, though it should be recorded that in the very early days, we, the society, when land values were still low, could have bought a large amount of nearby land for a modest figure, but nobody then, other than ourselves, had any notion that the shrine might one day expand and we could not persuade the authorities to buy it. Indeed the suggestion was met with the most incredible, and at the time, hurtful, derision. However, in 1970 it was a different story, and such acquisition of land was necessary and, when completed, a major step forward. The way was then clear to get on with building the church.

We were still in the era of no statues, and at a special council meeting in April 1970, we were informed by an impressive gathering of diocesan clerical experts and their architects that the new church and shrine would at last go ahead, and almost as an et cetera, an accepted fact, it was mentioned that the gable wall would be left bare. We could not believe what we were hearing but there, laid out for our examination, were the architects' plans, incorporating a bare gable. There was instant consternation among our members. We, the society, who for forty years had been talking about 'enhancing the gable' and for almost as many more had been collecting money for doing so, were now being asked for our views on plans which when completed, would present a bare wall to the people. It was a suggestion we could not accept. Indeed so strong were the objections from me and from all of us that day, that the plans were folded up and taken away, and that was an end of them. Everything was in abeyance for a while and none of us quite knew what to expect next. During those months Fr Horan was understandably non-committal when one met him. He had a great deal to do, and the whole question of the shrine was of course, very contentious. It seemed wiser for all concerned to let it rest for the moment and leave it all to God, and so it was. In November 1973, work began on the new church and huge improvements were undertaken around the grounds. It was as if some supernatural force drove Fr Horan to marathon undertakings. It was usual to see him quite late in the evening, his work with the pilgrims and builders done for that day, pacing round and round the grounds, his beads slipping through his fingers, as he said his rosary quietly to himself, but no doubt also laying new plans. Very soon he acquired a mobile telephone, a great novelty then, and with that permanently in his pocket, one wonders how much peace he got night or day; indeed that new and heavy stress was to be his fate for the rest of his life.

Work on the new church progressed steadily. Each *Annual* carried an editorial reminder of the approaching centenary, and each council meeting had words from all of us about the lack of plans for a shrine. In July 1976, the new church was finished, and, as with every new building that has been erected at Knock, it had the usual quota of scoffers, 'How will they fill it?' 'Another white elephant!', etc., but as it has turned out, the scoffers got it wrong. It was blessed by Cardinal Conway and fourteen bishops, while priests from every corner of Ireland came to concelebrate Mass, forming for the first time the now familiar great white circle around the altar as they did so. It was a day of radio, television and press coverage, but it was still only a new church. However, it was the first of many wonderful moments.

Very early that year, 1976, following hours and weeks of discussion with our council members, and realising that the time was then getting short, I made out an agenda for a meeting. There were three main items recorded, and they are still so recorded in the minutes of that meeting: 1. Invite the Holy Father for the centenary; 2. Invite foreign prelates; and 3. Make a request for the presentation of the Golden Rose. I was remembering all I had read and thought of way back in 1964, and now twelve years on, I was determined to try to get every possible honour and recognition for Knock for the centenary. The proposals made little impact at that meeting, Fr Horan had a knack of scanning an agenda and picking items which he was prepared to discuss, while he ignored all else. On that occasion he did just that.

I put them down again for a further meeting in November that same year. This time, knowing quite well that we would not give up, he studied the requests and said straight away that for such decisions we would have to ask the archbishop to be present, which was exactly the course of action we had expected. Without further delay, I sent an invitation to the archbishop, and the date for the next meeting was fixed for 4 December.

It turned out to be a day I shall never forget. Margaret Donnelly was staying with me in Bridgemount at the time, and on the morning of the meeting we awoke to one of the worst days of the winter. For some of the major events that have happened at Knock I seem to remember appalling weather conditions. Sometimes it looked as if all the forces of evil were gathering against us and that morning was no exception, it was intensely cold with thick freezing fog, reducing visibility to almost nil. After an early lunch we set out for Knock, my only concern being the real fear that nobody could manage to get there. The roads were icy and driving was very hazardous, but to our amazement, despite very long journeys for some, everybody turned up. All of our council members realised the importance of the occasion and, sensing the difficulties ahead perhaps, they all made the extra effort to get there. It was not a particularly long agenda, but it was a very important one for us. There were just the three main items with some minor matters for discussion, and we began. The archbishop arrived, took his place and looked quickly at the agenda, and that one quick glance was sufficient. Perhaps he may not have had enough notice of the suggestions, or he decided that we had overstepped the mark and taken too much upon ourselves, we shall never know, but he quickly made it clear that the business as set out, was the business of the bishops, and the bishops alone. This was something we already knew, we were merely asking to have these things done, but there was nothing he was prepared to consider or do about it just then and, without any further discussion, he left.

That ended the proceedings. We were all bitterly disappointed, and I wondered if our hoped-for, very special centenary would be relegated to being a minor event, making it just a national, rather than an international affair, as was then being mooted. However, all through my years at Knock I have never been put off by a refusal, there is always prayer, and on that occasion I prayed with all my heart. Next day I had to go to Knock for some reason and Margaret came with me. My business was in St Joseph's and I had some papers with me for somebody who was staying at the convent. As I was pressed for time I asked Margaret to take them there for me. Fr Horan, who by then had been made Canon Horan, also happened to be there at that precise moment and, seeing Margaret, he called her aside. He then told her that he had been trying to phone me without success, and asked her to take me a message, asking me to do nothing whatever about what had happened at the meeting the day before, and not to worry about it, just to leave things to him, and everything we had asked for would be done. He also asked her to assure me that the whole building project would be completed by 1978. Her business done, she returned to St Joseph's and gave me the message.

It sounded almost too much to hope for, and in the light of many years' experience of such situations, I wondered how it might be achieved. Yet as everybody knows now, it all came to pass. I expect that the challenge and scale of the project had its appeal. The canon had had time since the first meeting and even from the second, to consider the proposals, indeed they were no news to him even then, as we had talked about the like on several occasions. He had, in any event, probably decided for himself that the procedure was the right one, even before it came to committee stage. The suggestions were of course, unprecedented, and to a lesser man they would certainly have seemed very much out of order and probably excessive. He, however, was the God sent man for the moment, one who excelled in doing things on a grand scale and, come what may, on that occasion, he was going to try to accomplish it. God alone knows how he coped with everything, and what personal difficulties he had to encounter along the way, but as everybody knows, all was done.

That was in 1976, there was still a long way to go before our ambitions could materialise and we organised a fervent and determined campaign of prayer. It was a campaign of prayer just as intense as the one at the very beginning of our society. I, and indeed all of us, had numerous Masses offered for the Holy Souls, and they have never yet failed me. In the 1977 *Annual* editorial, readers were reminded that 'thousands of Irish people are already looking forward to taking part in what will be the greatest occasion in the history of Knock shrine since the Apparition took place in 1879' – as it turned out, they were prophetic words. In the same *Annual*, Canon Horan, in an article which he contributed, described plans for the Apparition gable and said, 'In this area we should have a representation of the Apparition that will show pilgrims at a glance what actually happened on that August evening in 1879'. At last, here was the first sign that the gable might be re-designed, as Canon Horan reiterated all we had been saying over and over again since 1935, over forty years before. At long last we seemed to be within sight of something significant.

From that moment on, Canon Horan never stopped. He was the builder supreme. We had had the new St Joseph's, then the new church, soon the new Rest and Care Centre for invalids, providing us with facilities we could never have believed possible, a very different scene from the seized up water taps and smoking stoves of our earlier years. Then came the amazing landscaping of the grounds, which completely transformed the whole place. I was almost afraid to enquire what he planned to do next as his momentum, it seemed, could not be halted. Now and then he would ring me with 'I am going to' mentioning something he had in his head and wait for a reaction. We would then talk about it, but once he got a notion, one could be fairly sure that it would be carried out. Sometimes it worked the other way, and I would say to him, 'Canon, what about doing?' Frequently the suggestion was rejected, often laughed at, but frequently too it was brought up again and was acted upon.

The centenary year dawned without a great deal of evidence that anything spectacular would happen. The archbishop wrote a foreword for the *Annual* paying tribute to our society and to the work it had done down the years in promoting the shrine, while Canon Horan in a separate article did much the same. He also listed the ceremonies and main events for the centenary year, the highlight of which was to be 'a day of special ceremonies on 15 August', without any elaboration as to what those ceremonies might be, at that stage he probably did not know himself. In the end, that turned out to be a very special day with most of the bishops of Ireland present. By then, he had told me confidentially, that the Pope had been invited during the previous year, but nobody could predict whether or not he might come. Indeed we all heard again and again that the idea was no more than a joke. The Pope would never come to Knock. Knock? Who ever heard of such nonsense!

All of that changed rapidly however, when on 21 July 1979, it was officially announced that he was coming. It was first heard on an early news flash on the BBC and immediately somebody phoned from London to tell me about it. Minutes afterwards RTÉ carried the announcement. There was then no doubt whatever about it. Pope John Paul II was coming to Knock for the centenary. It didn't take long to get things moving then. The bishops and priests all over the country, as by then all Ireland was involved, got together with commendable speed, and very quickly plans of action were drawn up. At Knock, the new church still needed some finishing, the grounds were new and raw, and the shrine, well, the shrine, something was by then being done about it. During all of this I wondered what the position would be about the statues, but as I have already said, when the boxes were opened, the contents were found to be perfect, gleaming white and spotless, as when they were first fashioned. Canon Horan worked with frantic speed, nobody giving him much encouragement as he laboured day and night to get the shrine built as well as to complete the thousand other things that still needed to be finished.

Meeting after meeting took place almost nightly. There was a little over nine weeks in which to organise everything. There were so many things that had to be considered. The archbishop was, of course, in charge of all operations, and, under him, several priests in the diocese, as well as expert lay people from all walks of life, each with a designated responsibility and committee, worked at full speed. There was transport, roads, communications, stewarding and marshalling of crowds, security, helpers, the sick, catering, the media, decoration and flowers. For the priests there was the liturgy, the music, the ministers, readers, cantors, the hundreds of priests who would be concelebrating, and the problem of finding vestments to clothe them, as well as the cardinals and bishops not to mention other VIPs and all the protocol concerning them. It was a gigantic undertaking, and inevitably several units and sub-units were organised to take charge of the various sections. Progress reports were exchanged all the time and despite apparent chaos now and then, everybody got on with it, and in the end, things miraculously came together. Those of us who were dealing with the sick and the helpers, often went on with our particular task at Knock until well past midnight, and then frequently Fr Frank Fahey, who was then CC there and working with us, would say morning Mass for us before we left for home in the small hours. It didn't seem worthwhile going to bed before we had to return for another round of talk.

Security was a very big problem, yet few on the outside were aware of it. Although it was a pastoral visit, the safety of the Pope was in the hands of the state, and the gardaí had to mount a massive security operation. All the helpers who were to be on duty on the day, all the expected sick, as well as the officiating priests and everybody required to be within a specific area, had to have their names, together with a picture, submitted for a check to the gardaí weeks in advance. Then an ID card was issued for every single one, and understandably, plenty of time was needed for this. Inevitably people wanted to be there, indeed as might be expected, some helpers who had not helped us very much down the years were the first to stake a claim and were most offended when this could not be arranged. Several people thought that they had only to write or phone and there would be no difficulty in getting into special places. I had a great deal of trouble from all of this, as it was almost impossible to get some people to appreciate the fact that space was very limited, and only those genuinely required as necessary and useful helpers could be admitted to this high security zone. I fear that a few people, and among them some friends of very long standing, have not yet forgiven me as I was not able to arrange to have them included. Even with all of that advance planning, I lost count of the number of times I was called out on the day of the Mass to identify handmaids who had been caught in impossible traffic, and because of the lateness of their arrival were held by security at the gates, even with their passes. However, it all went well despite the Pope's very long over-run in Galway and, at the end, the dismal rain which very nearly destroyed everything.

Predictably there were those who referred to the Pope's visit to Ireland without any reference to Knock, as if the reason for his coming was solely to visit Dublin or some place east of the Shannon. To several of the journalists who had travelled on the papal jet, Knock was a tiresome whimsy, somewhere out there in the west but a place that had to be visited. True, Dublin could lay on the Phoenix Park with its wide and welcoming spaces, the nunciature could be a haven for the tired Pontiff, there were comfortable hotels for the visitors and the roads in the capital could accommodate the expected volume of traffic with ease. Similarly, Drogheda, Galway and Limerick were big towns in their own right, used to large gatherings. Knock had no such facilities. A raw new church, newly landscaped and still far from finished grounds, narrow roads that could not easily cope with the inevitable inflow of traffic, it was not a particularly inviting place for such a visit. A very short time before the appointed day, Bishop Dominic Conway who was concerned about the success of the undertaking phoned me full of consternation. He had just driven through Knock and was dismayed by what he had seen. So bad had been his impression that he had stopped and gone into the grounds to check it as he didn't believe it to be possible. He found acres of rubble, JCBs and cement mixers all over the place, in short, chaos. Normally a reasonably pragmatic man, he was on this occasion quite anxious. Knock could never be ready for a papal visit, he told me, the whole thing would be a disgrace. I assured him that he was underestimating the man at the helm, that all would be finished as they were all working round the clock, and I begged him not to worry. Of course it was finished, but the effort involved, the day and night work and the strain of that colossal undertaking has rarely, if at all, been mentioned.

In remembering that centenary year, varied and often unconnected thoughts come back, it was all so incredible that it was difficult at the time to realise that it was happening. There will always be memories and images that one cannot forget, the landing of the Holy Father at Dublin airport. We had no time to watch it on television at Knock, but as we worked we listened to radios strategically planted. We heard about it as we fixed flowers, transfixed and silent, a handful of waxen blossoms in hand, prepared food for the sick, checked last minute plans, or stopped to swallow a sandwich. We had gone to Knock on the Friday afternoon, as all day on Saturday there was still so much to be done, and in any event, from then on the roads were choked, there was almost no getting there. Already the television vans were in place and setting up, the thousands of flowers had been delivered and were being arranged in the shrine and the church. Flower arrangement alone took over twenty-four hours, as bloom after bloom was individually fixed by numerous arrangers, viewed and examined from new vantage points high on television gantries above the altar, while more and still more flowers were added. Then on the Sunday, there was the endless wait as one delay after another was reported from Galway. The sick were already in the church, waiting, quietly tended by handmaids. There they stayed for the whole ceremony watching everything on huge monitor screens which had been erected all around the altar, high above the mountains of flowers. The open air Mass that had been so well planned, with its hundreds of white robed concelebrants carrying their silk-lined communion baskets fashioned from rushes, as they moved through the patient masses, and everywhere, away into the distance, that limitless expectant multitude standing patiently in the ever present drizzle.

As the evening shadows lengthened, I was gradually beginning to appreciate all that had happened. The new church had been raised to the status of Basilica and incredibly, the Golden Rose had been presented, and was there for all to see. The shrine had become a reality. The Holy Father had come to that shrine, and there, like any other pilgrim, he had knelt and prayed, then he lit a candle and blessed the statues. With tears very near my eyes I watched him do so while the television lights followed him, a warm circle of light in the blue dusk, poised just for a moment, before he was whisked away to his helicopter and off into the twilight, high above the sea of people who had travelled all through the night before to see him. As it had been on the night of the Apparition, so it was again, driving misty rain, but on this occasion again, nobody seemed to notice. The Pope had come to Knock for, as he had told us, 'the goal of my journey to Ireland', and Knock would never be the same again.

Perhaps it is worth recording at this stage that we first took notice of Knock in 1929 fifty years after the Apparition. Exactly fifty years later, Knock had received its ultimate recognition. Was it, one is tempted to ask yet again, coincidence? I do not think so. One of the legends current at the time about Canon Horan and Knock is that as he watched the Pope's helicopter lift off that night, he decided that the time had come for him to build an airport. He had thought about it off and on before that, but there never had been time. At last the moment seemed right, but again one asks, was all of this too the realisation of the original plans?

225

There is no need to tell again the saga of the airport, that theme was worked over and over again, until it became the standing joke for all occasions. Nevertheless, despite all odds, it was built, and built not just for pilgrim purposes, as we had first intended it to be, but to benefit the whole of the west of Ireland.

Canon Horan, who had become Monsignor Horan after the Pope's visit, saw his airport completed, and had the sweet pleasure of flying from it for the Golden Jubilee Pilgrimage to Rome of the Knock Shrine Society. In 1985, the whole of Connaught flocked to see the first jets take off for Rome carrying the Knock handmaids and stewards from their own airport. Captivated by the incredible story, the world's press were also there to record the event, tales of which appeared in the world's newspapers and television. Almost as if they had not believed what they had seen, the people of Connaught were there again to welcome us back, and give a rousing cheer to the incoming flights. Those planes were not a mirage, they were real, and friends alighted from them and came home to tell the tale. Meantime, we, the handmaids and stewards had been to Rome, several for the first time. Escorted by Monsignor Horan, Dr Cunnane, our bishop, Dr Conway, bishop of Elphin, Dr Flynn, bishop of Achonry , together with Monsignori P. Cremin, Maynooth, J. Hanly, Rector of the Irish College Rome, and T. Finnegan, later bishop of Killala, on the whole a strong contingent from the west, we were presented to the Holy Father. It was all very heady stuff at the time, and an undreamed of climax to all that had gone before. The following year Monsignor Horan flew from his airport again, this time to Lourdes, and as everybody knows, he did not see his homeward journey. In the twinkling of an eye, Our Lady called him to herself while he slept, for what must have been for him, the perfect homecoming.

In the disbelief that followed the announcement of his death, few could imagine it possible: the man who had built the Basilica, and built an airport, had been called away from us. Thinking about it however, it is not difficult to realise the reason. Beneath the determined, often jocose and seemingly solid exterior, he was still only human. The superhuman effort that went into all that building, the responsibility, the fundraising, constant travelling, relentless publicity and being the butt of wounding jokes and sarcasm from lesser people, inevitably took its toll. True, he always got the better of his opponents, whether television presenters or politicians, but who can estimate the cost to himself? For us, however, and for researchers when the full history of the shrine comes to be written, he will always remain the man who was responsible for building the present day Knock. Without doubt, he was chosen specially by Our Lady to do so, a gigantic assignment which he carried out superbly.

15

Priests through the years
Work today

S ometimes, as I sit in the Basilica and watch the lines of white robed priests as they file in to begin Mass, I re-call what it was like in the early days, and often wonder if I am dreaming or if all I am seeing is real. Today, people would find it difficult to realise that when we began to pro-mote Knock, very few priests believed in the Apparition, and their response to us, the lay people, was at best, tole-rant, but more usually, it was hostile. There were occasions while working at the shrine when I was asked by a priest whom I hadn't seen for some time, 'Are *you* still here?' as if our involvement was expected to be some sort of passing whim. Occasionally, one got the more honest comment which presumably reflected the more dominant thought, 'What do you expect to get out of this?' There were many times when we decided that we could take no more, and on such occasions we would go to Tuam to whichever arch-bishop happened to be there to tell him so, only to be per-suaded by him to carry on for a little longer. This happened with almost all of the bishops, and so we continued on and on.

In these post conciliary years, involvement of the laity in Church affairs has become accepted as normal up to a point, but in the mid-1930s a very different attitude pre-vailed. The laity then had little or no voice, the business of the Church was the business of the bishops and the priests, they made the decisions and there the matter rested. In the case of Knock, we were dealing with something quite unique;

nothing comparable had ever come within the jurisdiction of the Irish Church, and so, understandably, it was treated with extreme caution. As far as we, the laity, were concerned however, the case for its full recognition by the Church was clear-cut and had more convincing evidence to support its claim than many shrines worldwide where ecclesiastical approval had been given. All that said, it would be next to impossible for anybody today to imagine the difficulties we had to encounter at the beginning, something we were to experience slowly and often very painfully.

With the benefit of hindsight, it is always easier to take a balanced view, and, putting it in perspective today, I suppose that such a response was to be expected, as in general, reports of apparitions are not normally regarded by the clergy with great favour. The Church authorities had moved cautiously at Lourdes, and indeed everywhere else. In the case of Knock, there was the added problem of the then fairly recent history of Sr Mary Frances Cusack, the Nun of Kenmare. Few people remember her name now, but it was not always so. In her day she had been a well-known writer, a convert to Catholicism who came to Knock as a Poor Clare sister from her convent in Kenmare. The story of her time at Knock is a turbulent one, moving from being the close friend of the parish priest, Archdeacon Cavanagh, at the beginning, to becoming at the end, the avowed enemy of the archbishop, Dr McEvilly, and other clerics. Finally, she left Knock and, eventually, the Church. In her early writings she defended the Apparition very firmly, she also raised large sums of money for the poor during times of great hardship and made an effort to provide badly needed schools, something for which priests and people were grateful. However, despite her brilliant mind and her great charitable achievements, she created a deep feeling of bitterness, a bitterness which lingered for far too long, as even at the time we began our work, the name of Knock was synonymous with hers, generating considerable suspicion and resentment. She was a resolute woman much maligned, who was years ahead of her time, yet she was, without doubt, one of the reasons for at least some of the clerical animosity.

There were stories of one parish priest who had been at Knock some years before our time, who had given instructions to have crutches which had been left at the shrine in thanksgiving for cures, burned. Leading up to the Second Commission of Enquiry in 1936, when everything about the Apparition was being analysed and questioned in depth, Canon Grealy was quite emphatic that the only objection he had ever heard to its authenticity had come from the priests. He told us later that as far as he was concerned, and it was a point he wanted to stress, all the objections had come from people who had never bothered to enquire into its history at all. He also made it clear that because of that ignorance, or more realistically, indifference, he did not consider their attitudes to be worthy of notice.

It would be difficult now to decide when exactly a change in attitude came about, it was gradual and almost imperceptible for years. All of the bishops were, without exception, sympathetic to Knock. Dr Gilmartin, who was the first to take any positive action about it, did so after much personal prayer and heart searching, and then it was directly in response to our approach. Dr Walsh, who followed him, was a firm supporter, and came on pilgrimage regularly, leading the diocese every year. He was a very approachable man, who dealt with matters in a forthright manner regardless of what people might have thought. I still have several of his letters in my desk, always handwritten in green ink. When the telephone came into general use he would call me himself when he needed to discuss something, never through an intermediary. In his years as archbishop, almost thirty of them, the renewal at Knock was firmly set in place and the ground work completed, so from then on it was mainly a matter of ongoing development.

As far as the priests generally were concerned, several remained sceptical for years, but there was the occasional one who was sympathetic from the beginning. I clearly remember one parish priest who brought a group of pilgrims to Knock regularly, perhaps his parishioners arranged it and he went along with them, or perhaps he made the going, I don't know, but in any event, he came. At the end of each visit he would come to us and whisper, 'How are you getting on?' and when we told him that things were progressing, he would say, 'Keep up the good work, but don't tell anyone I said so'. Such an attitude gives an idea of the climate then prevailing. Any support had to be in secret and, given a whiff of disapproval on any front, it would have been withdrawn very quickly.

It would be quite wrong, however, to give the impression that all priests were unsympathetic, far from it. All through the years, there have been notable exceptions and, in turn, we valued those men and their sound advice on all matters, greatly. The first was Fr Jarlath Ronayne, the Cistercian whom I have already mentioned at length in relation to Mrs Morrin and his visit to us at Bridgemount. Fr Jarlath was born into a very comfortably-off family and at an early age he decided to become a priest. When he was first ordained, his father with natural paternal pride, bought him a thoroughbred hunter, as being a very competent horseman, he loved to ride in his free time. Very soon, however, he grew tired of this relatively easy life, as he gradually realised that he had not yet found fulfilment within it, and that something more might yet be required of him.

After much heart searching he began to feel a strong urge to join an enclosed order and decided to approach the

Cistercians at Roscrea. He told us of the bitter opposition to this decision he had to endure from his family, and of his own anguish on having to hurt them, an anguish that continued to plague him during his early years in the monastery. In his loneliness, he suffered greatly, but eventually he found solace in his devotion to the way of the cross. During his stay with us he gave us valuable information about the old Knock which he remembered from days very shortly after the Apparition. He told us of the faith of the people then, of their stark poverty, and of the enormous pilgrimages which came there. He instilled into our minds a realisation that we were doing something very necessary and, despite his gentle approach, maybe because of it, he generated a strong sense of purpose within us increasing our determination to carry on. In those, our early faltering days, this enthusiastic encouragement meant a great deal to us.

Very much in the same mould, yet very different in manner, was Fr Angelus, OFM, Cap. He too was one of our first friends, and that friendship lasted for his lifetime. Some people will still remember Fr Angelus of the Reek. Every Reek Sunday he came to Westport and climbed the Reek, even when he had grown to be an old man. He was always to be seen there, whatever the weather, climbing with the best of them, his long brown habit blowing in the wind of the bleak mountain. He came to Knock to preach in the very early days and he defended it on a couple of occasions when a very influential clerical critic was fulminating against it. He would come to stay with us and make light of all our worries. He had known my sister Marie in Dublin when she was first married and, through her, had got to know me when I was a young girl. He had a wonderful sense of humour which transcended the varying problems, but one could always rely on him for trenchant comment and defence when necessary. In one of the early *Annuals*, there is a picture of him preaching at Knock, his long Capuchin beard falling full behind an old fashioned round microphone. It was, as I remember it, a great sermon!

At that time too, we first met Fr Benedict, ODC. He had been a pupil of Fr Jarlath's, and Fr Jarlath with his customary kindness, had asked him to write an article for us for the *Annual*, when articles were not all that easy to come by, especially from priests. Fr Benedict did, and he continued to contribute to it for the rest of his life, mostly in Irish. A fluent Gaelic speaker and scholar, he was responsible for organising the first Irish-speaking pilgrimage. As we got to know him better, he grew to be a staunch personal friend. He frequently came to stay with us on his way to or from the Aran Islands, the place that was to him a paradise on earth. He and Liam would talk in Irish for half the night and loved to exchange stories. It was no use trying to disturb them, or tell them that the hour for sleeping had come, and frequently gone. Engrossed in their Aran Irish they forgot time and place, but it was such a tonic to both of them, that to interrupt them would have been cruel. Each time we went to Dublin, Fr Benedict came round to our hotel to meet us and we would talk for hours, time totally forgotten. He would then get up to leave us and cycle home – he cycled everywhere. He was known and loved by many people, in particular the poor. When he died I missed him sorely, as I had come to rely on him for his valued advice in many things. For all of that, and for his many contributions to the *Annual*, I shall always be grateful.

Sometime in the late 1930s, we first met the two irrepressible brothers, Dr Pat and Dr Michael O'Carroll of the Holy Ghost Order. They were very young priests when they first came to Knock on some Dublin pilgrimage and we soon singled them out as being very special indeed. We met Fr Pat first, as Fr Michael, then considerably younger, was still a post graduate student at the university in Fribourg. Fr Pat stayed with us many times; he was open and generous minded, and we could talk to him freely about our problems. Blessed with a keen sense of humour, he would listen to us and then, when remedies had been suggested, and the problem more or less resolved, at least in theory, he would proceed to reduce everything to fun. It was a wonderful antidote, and restored equilibrium when humour was probably the only remedy. I remember how we used to sit in the study till all hours at night listening wide-eyed to stories of his incredible encounters, but always ending with laughter, then we would all, very reluctantly, climb the stairs to bed. In sharp contrast to all of that, he was a deeply spiritual man with a keen analytical brain. He too sent us splendid articles when such a gesture meant a great deal. At a very early age, he was made Provincial of the Holy Ghost Order, and soon after that went abroad for several years. Unfortunately, while working in America, he died when far too young, but he is somebody I shall always remember with gratitude and affection.

In the beginning, his brother, Dr Michael seemed to be very different and much more serious-minded, but beneath all his great scholarship, he is a most light-hearted man. Probably the greatest expert today on Marian doctrine, he has written scholarly books on the subject, definitive works which have taken several years of research in libraries all over the world. Yet it is good to know that he is almost always at the end of the telephone, and so it has always been. All through the years, whether my query was something trivial or something requiring great knowledge, judgement and frequently diplomacy, he has always been approachable and generous with advice. He gave us our first handmaids' and stewards' Day of Recollection many years ago, when our venue was one of the old wooden huts and our numbers were a couple of dozen. Over the years since then, he has, despite a very heavy personal writing commitment, contributed generously to the *Annual*, preached frequently at the shrine, and he still remains a true and valued friend

One day a letter arrived in the post and enclosed were a few stamps to cover the cost of an *Annual*. In those days the *Annual* cost a couple of shillings, if even that, and the request had come from a Capuchin called Fr Hubert. We sent him the *Annual*. It was, as far as I remember, only the second or maybe third edition, and after a little time, a correspondence began between us. Gradually, we got to know him, and before long he was himself contributing articles regularly and we were soon to find in him a most valuable friend. He wrote a lot on Knock, as apart from his articles, he did numerous booklets on various aspects of the Apparition. He also wrote a massive work which took several years of intensive research, on devotion to the Holy Souls.

Fr Hubert would come to stay with us off and on during the season. He always loved walking and would walk alone for hours out on the bog road, rhapsodising over the flowers and the birdsong while he meditated or maybe said his Office. In those days one heard the constant call of the cuckoo and the corncrake, and in the twilight, the eerie sound of the *mionan aerac* or jacksnipe, haunted the western skies. Totally immersed in the beauties of nature, he was oblivious to the wind and the rain, so it was not unusual to find him returning to the house his long brown habit drenched from a sudden shower. That was in the days before central heating, when drying any wool garment was a real problem, though he rarely even noticed his drenching. Fr Hubert went to God some years ago, but he is remembered by all of us with great affection.

I have already written at length about the valued friendship of Dr Dominic Conway, who, since he first wrote to us as a young priest in the early 1950s, when I most needed a real friend, showed kindness and concern beyond measure. It was always good to know that, even when the business of his diocese made heavy demands on his time, one could always call on him for advice and he was never slow in responding.

During the early years of our work we were fortunate in finding a good friend in Dr James Fergus, who was then secretary to the archbishop. We always found him to be a sympathetic intermediary when we went to Tuam and his advice was most valuable. A quiet, droll man, he kept things in the archbishop's establishment moving smoothly, and at times, when we called there full of despair, our minds quite made up to drop everything, he invariably found some humourous angle to the situation and sent us home with much lighter hearts, the crisis of the moment put into perspective. As diocesan censor he was most helpful with advice and suggestions when proposed publications were submitted. Later, as parish priest of Ballinrobe he was unfailing in his support for Knock, and later still, as bishop of Achonry, he never forgot to come into the invalids' section to see me when he came to Knock with his pilgrimage. Such gestures, small though they may seem today, were a tremendous boost to morale in those days.

In his own way too, Dr Gilmartin, our archbishop, could also be considered to have been a friend, as from the beginning he was very concerned about the difficulties we were encountering at so many levels. Generally he said little, and we knew that he could not reasonably become too involved, but his encouragement all along indicated his genuine sympathy and approval for our work.

The priests from the SMA College in Ballinafad called on us regularly during those days, and among them Fr Harry Sheppard who was superior there for a time was always available to listen and to counsel wisely. Around the same time we got to know Fr Jim Byrne, a gentle soul, who spent a great part of his later life working in Africa. He was a very saintly man who, up to a very short time before his death a few years ago, wrote regularly for us. Though he died at a relatively early age, he suffered a great deal in later years, but he bore it without complaint, serenely.

In more recent times, the late Fr Berchmans, a Cistercian from Mellifont Abbey, was a priest of sterling quality. I met him some time after I got back from Rome in 1960. When I was with Sr Perpetua Hayes in Naples she mentioned him to me as somebody who was very interested in Knock and I seem to remember that I met him, quite by accident, shortly after that, and from the beginning, he was somebody very special. He wrote regularly for the *Annual*: deep spiritual pieces on varied matters, which he frequently signed 'A Monk from Mellifont'. His devotion to the Blessed Sacrament was remarkable, and assisting at his Mass was a profound experience. Over the years he was most generous when he came to Knock in saying Mass for us in St Brigid's, the handmaids' house, and that Mass was a source of great inspiration to all of us. He had great devotion to the shrine and he delighted in exploring the vast canvas of the Apparition, highlighting its various aspects from time to time. His later discourses were on the importance of the Lamb in the vision, the only place in the world where the Lamb of God has been seen. News of his death, after a very short illness came to us quite unexpectedly and we, the Knock family of handmaids, and I in particular, miss him, even yet.

The present parish priest, Monsignor Dominick Grealy, who was appointed directly after Monsignor Horan, was faced with a huge task, having suddenly to take on work that was intended for both of them. It was a tremendous challenge, but he is coping wonderfully well and has continued the expansion of the shrine with the building of the magnificent Apparition Chapel and the Chapel of Reconciliation, each one splendid in its own way. He is a quiet, shy man who sees things that need to be done and does them. Above all else, he is determined to make Knock a very holy place and his insistence on silence within the shrine precinct will do much to call attention to, and highlight, its silent message.

Now and then during the early years we had several very amusing encounters with priests, which made a very pleasant change from the normally serious routine. Those incidents were never meant to be funny but somewhere along the way, something happened to make them so. Early in the campaign it was decided that we would have to look in every locality in the west for men to act as stewards, and so, with due deference and formality, we sought and received permission from all the Connaught bishops to enlist such men from their various dioceses. Having secured this permission, which was given in all cases without any hesitation, we assumed that everything necessary had been done, and the time had come for action.

For our first approach we chose a priest who was then a high-ranking cleric in our own archdiocese, and as Liam had a heavy schedule of courts coming up, we thought that I might as well make a start on my own. Hardly anybody had a telephone in those days and the question of making a written appointment, other than with a bishop or somebody equally elevated, did not cross one's mind. People called on each other quite casually and thought nothing about it. The day chosen to begin was warm and sunny, so I put on a white linen suit, a wide brimmed white straw hat, high heeled white shoes and in my bag, I had my letter of authorisation! By today's standards, I would be dressed for a wedding or maybe a garden party, but in the 1930s, such an outfit, even to the hat, would have been normal enough on a very warm day, and warm days came as rarely then as now, so one made the most of them.

Quite happy with myself and the worthiness of my mission, I drove to the priest's house, parked my car in the drive, got out and rang the bell. Nothing happened and I rang again. After what seemed to be an eternity the door was opened about two inches and a woman's face showed through the chink. She sized me up from head to toe, and then with obvious disdain enquired curtly what I wanted. I told her that I had come to see the parish priest, but she lost no time in informing me that I could not do that without first telling her my business. Realising that I would make no progress without appearing at least to do so, I outlined briefly the reason for my call. She thought about it for a moment, then, no doubt classing me as a cheeky piece who would not go away, I was told to wait, while the door was firmly shut. Again I waited for ages, and eventually she returned. This time she opened the door a few inches and I was instructed, not asked, to come in.

Inside the door there was a tiny alcove, big enough to accommodate a single coat, or maybe a small child, and I was curtly instructed to wait in there and not to move. The minutes ticked away and after a positive age, the priest himself came along. Now it was his turn to look me over, while the housekeeper stood at the back of the hall at a safe distance, but perfectly positioned to hear every word that was said. I was now questioned about my business, which this time I told a little more fully, though by then I was beginning to realise that I was not particularly welcome at any level. He listened to me with obvious contempt, then he drew himself up to his full height and let me know in very clear terms what he thought about Knock, and it wasn't very much.

Suddenly, as I had said absolutely nothing, he ran out of steam and stopped. With a face scarlet from annoyance at the uncalled for intrusion, he asked me curtly what I had said my name was. I told him. He paused and asked again, and I again told him. As realisation dawned, the effect was electric. He muttered that of course I couldn't possibly be any relation to Liam, and when I assured him that I was, in fact I was his wife, he was covered with confusion. I was invited at once to come in, to have tea, or something to wet my lips. By that stage it was my turn to get mad, my temper had begun to rise and I was just about to say so, when there was a final plea to 'come in and see the canary', obviously the ultimate treat! That finished me, and put an end to my, by then, genuine annoyance. From that moment, I had problems trying to hide my amusement, as the situation became even funnier. I have forgotten how I finally extricated myself, but I did, and on the surface at least, we appeared to be firm friends. The story had a happy ending however, as that poor man came to Knock the following Sunday to help, and the Sunday after, and for many Sundays for the rest of his life, so in the end, some good came out of it, even if it was a very long time before the subject of stewards was mentioned again in that particular parish.

Those were the days of innocence and sincere unquestioning faith, and I often wonder how we would fare if the question of Knock's, or indeed any shrine's promotion were to arise today. Even if one or two people could be found who would be prepared to devote the time to the work, could the same result now be achieved? Somehow I think it would still take a comparable amount of effort, but I hope I am wrong.

Each season ends as it began, with the Day of Recollection for handmaids and stewards, and as we all say goodbye for the winter, many of them say to me 'It will be nice for you now, you can get a few months' rest'. Very few, even among the well-informed handmaids and stewards, know what the winter entails, and has always entailed for me. It is the time for taking stock, for thinking about plans for the new season, for council meetings, for enlisting new helpers, and for dealing with any new publications by our society, in particular it means the *Annual*. The *Annual* was first planned to be a complete record of everything that happens at the shrine during the year, and as it now stands, it is the only source of historical facts. It carries articles of current interest, and it lists all pilgrimages which came during the year, together with their preachers, organisers and choirs. Without it, a great deal of this information would have been lost, but with recorded dates for everything, it has proved to be an invaluable tool through the years, answering enquiries of all kinds. To facilitate its use it now badly needs an index and if the Lord spares me I hope to persuade an indexer, perhaps as a thesis for a degree, to complete one.

It is planned in late autumn, then articles are sought from contributors and a general listing prepared. Having received the typescripts they must be edited, then as soon as the first proofs come from the printer, they are corrected. This is a demanding and slow task, as print errors are usual at that stage but cannot be tolerated in the final print-off, so the job requires a great deal of patience and concentrated work. Should one be thinking of using material already in print or published during the past fifty or, these days, even more, years, copyright must be cleared and the author's permission obtained. This is the law, but it is no more than common courtesy; it is nice to record that nobody has ever refused us permission to quote. It could be annoying to say the least, to find work which was prepared with care and considerable effort, used casually by somebody else without permission, or even more so, without even a mention of source. I fear it happens from time to time.

One afternoon somebody bearing the highest recommendation came by arrangement to Bridgemount to make in depth enquiries about the shrine. As his credentials were impeccable, I had set the time aside for him, gave him a meal and then talked to him at length, asking him several times about the reason for his interest, but was assured that it was solely because he wanted to be clear on every detail. However, I had my doubts, as his questioning was very precise, too precise for any purpose other than writing. In the end, as apart from anything else, I had got tired talking, I gave him copies of relevant publications and he left. Several months later I saw the results of that encounter in print, with not even a mention of his source. Such is the courtesy awarded to one now and then, but not too often I am pleased to say, people are not normally so blatantly ill-mannered.

Pictures must then be chosen, each year there are numerous new pictures of people and events at the shrine, and a choice must be made from them for use. Finally there are frequent consultations with the printer to decide about layout until the *Annual* is ready to print off, when a copy is sent to Tuam to get the archbishop's official permission, the *Imprimatur*. It is a demanding and very time-consuming job which takes quite a few months through the winter and into early spring to be in time for the opening pilgrimage in April. I had the honour of editing the *Knock Shrine Annual* for fifty-eight years, and during those years I saw many changes. A few years ago, realising that continuity was important, and that it was becoming difficult for me for many reasons, I asked Mr Tom Neary, the chief steward at Knock, if he would consider taking it on. This he very kindly consented to do, and he has done so now for some years, and done it very well. He has wide experience in writing with several worthwhile books on the shrine to his credit. He gives valuable organisational expertise to the shrine and I, above anybody else, know the demands the *Annual* will make on him, yet he does it with great grace, and no doubt will take it to a standard undreamed of through the years.

Each year also, we have applications from women who wish to become handmaids. Nobody is taken casually on application, each one has to be recommended in writing by another handmaid, and as the standards required are high, each application gets a great deal of checking. I appreciate that the handmaids' contribution is voluntary, and there are some who would argue that because of this, we should be more lenient. However, I have always taken the view that the work is for Our Lady, and as such, only work of the highest quality is good enough. On the practical level also, it is quite impossible to run anything properly if organisation is slipshod, or there is any doubt about the reliability or quality of the help available. On the other side of the coin, helpers would not thank one if having taken the trouble to come on duty, and sacrificed their free day, they found no specific duties outlined, or no clear instructions given as to the standards expected from them when carrying out those duties. Since nothing of any merit is ever achieved easily or without a good measure of planning, it is inevitable that running the handmaids or the stewards demands a high degree of commitment. In these days of easily accessible technology and computers it would be relatively easy to list helpers on a disc, and call or cancel them at the touch of a key. Of course it is in theory, these developments can certainly make things easier physically, but it never has been, nor will it ever be, just a question of making a list. One has to take into account the human element, where everybody must be evaluated and related to the work which might be allocated to them. It all takes time, thought, and experience; even then, nobody can guarantee perfection.

When we began our work for Knock we were young and several who came to work with us were young too, but we had strength to carry out hard work, and vision to plan for the future. Today, as I look around me at the young people, I am full of admiration for their warm, caring and positive attitudes. Their minds are open and receptive, and they in turn have a lot to contribute. I am sad that I am no longer young to work beside them, but I know that the flower of them, who come to join our ranks as handmaids and stewards, will contribute their own special talents and expertise to add a new dimension to our apostolate. They are the future, they have valuable ideas and standards of their own to contribute, and in so doing, they in turn will find the spiritual meaning for which they secretly long.

A great deal of thought and planning goes into the organisation of the Days of Recollection. With well over a thousand voluntary helpers, spiritual directors for all these varied people are, in consultation with the Knock priests, chosen with care. Notices are prepared and distributed, and for the spring day, when we don't have a working day to meet each other in advance, a notice is posted to every helper. In fairness to all of them, both handmaids and stewards, they turn up faithfully and enthusiastically, and it is always good to see them at the beginning of each season, and to wonder together what the year might bring.

In the autumn and in the spring, the council of the Knock Shrine Society has meetings. For these the parish priest is present, since in all major matters relating to the shrine he is the ultimate authority. Prior to those meetings, however, comprehensive discussion and analysis of the previous season takes place, mostly on the telephone. There are times when I feel sorry for anybody trying to contact me while these discussions are taking place, as they can go on for ages. All our council members appreciate the importance of this consultation and since the search continues all the time for ways to improve things, each agenda receives maximum time and thought. Then, regardless of weather conditions in winter, which can sometimes be quite awful, members do not hesitate to make the very long journeys which some of them have to undertake to get to these meetings.

I often wonder if the average pilgrim who comes to the shrine stops for a moment to consider the enormous amount of work that is necessary to make that pilgrimage day a success. Before they even set out, the pilgrimage organisers will have booked their place with the shrine authorities probably a year, certainly several months in advance, to ensure that they can be accommodated on that day, then they will advertise it in the relevant publicity outlets, and endeavour to fill the trains and buses they have booked to take them. They may have to find a preacher to accompany them, also a choir, and most of them arrange for invalids to be taken, who in turn will have to be escorted by suitable helpers. Then, having got to the shrine, participated in their devotions and all that goes with them and probably had something to eat, they have to get them home again, no doubt encountering some problem pilgrims who may have to be seen safely home well past the pick up point.

At Knock, the handmaids and stewards will have been on duty since early morning making ready for the crowds, and in turn the priests and staff at the shrine office will have sorted out the order of ceremonies and their celebrants. Then as the devotions begin there are endless responsibilities which continue right through the afternoon: the Mass, the Anointing and Blessing of the Sick, and the

245

Procession. All of these need careful thought and organisation to ensure that everything is carried out smoothly and without a hitch. It is always edifying to see Holy Communion distributed to thousands of people in the Basilica by a positive legion of priests, handmaids and stewards, as well as other ministers of the Eucharist, within a few minutes, and always with devotion and reverence.

Behind the scenes the sacristan will have laid out dozens of sets of vestments, as well as sacred vessels and all the other articles necessary for the service. The organist and choir, already well-rehearsed will be in position, and as the priests' procession comes in to begin the ceremonies, everything will have been attended to and every eventuality carefully considered. Strategically placed throughout the Basilica, trained handmaid nurses and stewards experienced in first aid wait quietly in case of emergency or illness, while another batch are ready in St John's to receive any such casualties. Emergencies happen from time to time, but they are dealt with efficiently and quietly, and a doctor called when necessary, almost unnoticed by the general congregation.

All through the morning the local priests together with several who are visiting and helping out have been hearing confession, which has now become almost an integral part of each pilgrimage, and pilgrims are happy to avail of the facility. Providing confession at Knock is an enormous responsibility for the priests as there is a never-ending stream of penitents, so numerous confessors must be available to deal with them. It begins early in the morning and goes on right into late afternoon, and in the month of August, early evening. It is a source of constant amazement to learn of the numbers who have partaken of this sacrament.

And so each season comes and goes, each one bringing its own problems and solutions, very different for us today from those which presented themselves in the 1930s, yet basically, as far as the pilgrims go, the problems are very much the same. People come to Knock to pray, whether it be for better health, better living conditions, better relationships, or sometimes, even better weather. Frequently there are those who come to give thanks. Giving thanks is very much part of our devotion, especially for the few of us who have been privileged to see Knock grow since we first saw it with wondering eyes all those years ago. It is no longer a poor village on the edge of civilisation, forgotten by all but a few. Today it takes its place among the great shrines of the world, as people from every country in that world gradually come to know about it and, like all of us when they at last discover it, marvel at the splendour, the richness and the majesty of its unique apocalyptic Apparition.

Epilogue

This book was put together over many years in sessions with Judy Coyne, given very reluctantly whenever time permitted. Looking at it now, even after the few months since completion, and meantime, having examined hundreds of her letters and documents, it is quite obvious that, despite her colourful and graphic description of events, it is not even half the picture. It has become very clear that she told each story with the absolute minimum of focus on her personal action; she never looked on any development at Knock as in any way arising from her efforts, though in truth, without those efforts, these things would not have happened.

It would be impossible for me to put her in perspective, or to assess her importance in the development of the shrine and the potential of its rapidly expanding hinterland. Even more difficult for me would be to quantify the importance of the unprecedented lay involvement in Church affairs, particularly bearing in mind the structure and thinking of the Church in this country in the 1930s, 1940s and indeed until relatively recent times. However, it is clear from her own telling and from the obvious expansion of all aspects of the shrine, that Judy Coyne and her Knock Shrine Society Council colleagues made a huge contribution to the Church in this country long before the Second Vatican Council requested more lay participation. From childhood, I was well aware of the part she was playing, and know that from the moment she became involved with Knock, every hour of her every day was devoted to its promotion, no matter what the sacrifices, and they were many.

Nobody outside a very small circle knew the extent of her involvement, and few realise today that because of her vision, her pioneering expertise and courageous determination, the small almost forgotten shrine which she and her husband, Liam, were inspired to promote after their seemingly accidental visit there in 1929, would grow to what it now is: huge, important and respected, with its unique Apparition Chapel, its Basilica, its airport and, above all, that extraordinary visit to it by the Pope. Most people know of the Pope's visit to Ireland in 1979, few will realise that it came about through the dream and determination of this woman who, in 1964, reading in the morning paper of the visit of Pope Paul VI to the Holy Land and his stated intention to visit other Marian shrines, decided then and there that he should be invited to Knock for its centenary, and at once began an all out campaign to have this done. Going through her papers recently I came across a bundle of newspapers tied loosely in ribbon. They were colour supplements to several continental daily papers with lavish picture spreads covering that Holy Land visit. From that moment, a visit by the Pope to Knock for its centenary was the first item on all her council meetings agendas. So it was that the Pope's visit to Ireland came about, first and foremost in response to an invitation to Knock – 'the goal of my journey to Ireland'. Nobody will ever know of her struggle to bring this about, or the derision she endured, silently, even to the moment of the papal landing.

In the same way today, as our jet thunders for take off, or levels out for landing on the magnificent runway at Knock Airport, few will realise that at the first meeting of the Knock Shrine Society back in 1935, one of the items on the agenda was 'The provision of an airstrip for pilgrims' an item that caused its share of ridicule in its day, but which, like everything else on that agenda, she lived to see completed.

She always avoided publicity, and having achieved each goal, stood back to get on with the next project and let others take the credits. Newspapers, radio and television tried time and again to interview her, but she would have none of it. Around the time of the Pope's visit she answered the telephone one morning, it was Monsignor Horan and he calmly announced 'We're coming over'. In a response to the question 'Who are *we*?' she was told, 'Me and the BBC'. Glancing through the window at the same moment she saw the television caravans drawing up outside. It didn't take long to set them on their way again, without an interview. That was only one of the numerous occasions when she quietly walked away. I knew of many, many more.

In mid December 2001, I came back to Bridgemount to spend Christmas with her as I had done for many years. She welcomed me warmly as always, full of good spirits and news about all that was happening, but she appeared to be very tired. However, I soon realised that with her efficient and much valued secretary, Mary Devoy, she had just completed her annual task of sending several hundred Christmas cards to handmaids, promoters, family and friends, so I put the tiredness down to that and thought no more about it.

Then on Christmas Day as we drove home from Mass, she wondered out loud if she had done her last season in Knock, and who, among the handmaids, would she ask to take over from her. The days wore on and she prayed constantly for direction, not that there was anything new in that, her whole life was a prayer from the moment she rose at five each morning, until she closed her eyes, usually around midnight. It would be safe to say that nobody, not even close family or friends, realised the depth of her spirituality. Those of us who were very close to her often said that no priest or nun, even from enclosed orders lived a life of such dedication and prayer. Those priests and nuns had their recreation, their time off, maybe even the occasional holiday, she never allowed herself any of these. Now, however, she was praying even more earnestly for direction, wondering who among the handmaids she should choose. After much thought and deliberation she picked six to take on different responsibilities, the things she had been doing single-handedly all her life. Having made her choice she phoned each one of them or had them visit her at Bridge-mount in an effort to persuade them, and each in turn eventually agreed to her proposals. She then wrote to Monsignor Grealy, at that time parish priest, telling him of her arrangements, and he replied expressing approval, but hoping for her continuing involvement and guidance at the heart of things.

On receipt of that letter she wrote another, her last, this time to the general body of handmaids, telling them what she had done and asking for their co-operation. She signed it, it was copied and posted at once to about five hundred handmaids.

Next morning, Holy Thursday, she collapsed as she came downstairs; she was exhausted, spent. The few weeks that remained to her were a revelation. She was at peace, happy in the knowledge that her life's work was finished and blessing beyond all others, she was satisfied that she had chosen her successors wisely, and that her work at Knock would continue to be carried out in accordance with God's plan. It was a serene and beautiful ending to a life that was lived in the belief that 'nothing happens by chance, there is a Providence in everything' and above all to a life completely devoted to the promotion of the wondrous Apparition at Knock with the Lamb of God as its centrepiece, an image unique in the entire world.

She now rests re-united with her beloved Liam in a quiet corner of the old cemetery at Knock, where, surrounded by birdsong and the echo of prayers and hymns wafted to them on the quiet air from the pilgrim path below, they watch over the realisation of their dream which, together, in the fullness of youth, 'with Providence their guide' they set out to achieve seventy-three years before.

Ethna Kennedy
Bridgemount, November 2003

Index of Names

The Spirit of Tony de Mello
John Callanan SJ

A book which captures the essence and spirit of Tony de Mello. Callanan begins with a chapter on the basics of prayer; and moves on to try and give a flavour of the ideas and themes which gave so much life to de Mello's presentations. The book includes exercises based on the prayer-style which de Mello developed during hs retreats.

Woman in Search of Wholeness
Anne Alcock

A book for use in personal prayer, small prayer groups, private retreats and quiet days. It combines insights from the Bible with short reflections on life themes. It also provides a series of relaxation and visualisation exercises.

Irish Saints
Peg Coghlan

The Island of Saints and Scholars was aptly named and produced hundreds of true saints from the fifth to the ninth century. This book provides select biographies of the men and women whose sanctity, austerity, humanity and scholarship are the glory of Irish history, including Patrick, Brigid, Brendan, Columcille and Ailbe.